Teresa K. Lasher

LIFE IS:
Good
Fragile
Precious

LOVING YOURSELF SO YOU CAN LOVE OTHERS

Life is: Good, Fragile, Precious

Copyright © 2016 Teresa K. Lasher

ISBN-13: 978-1532718342

Names: Teresa K. Lasher, author.

Title: *Life is; Good, Fragile, Precious: Loving yourself so you can love others*

Subjects: Lasher, Teresa K./Devotional–Meditation/Spiritual Living/Health-related issues/Christian Biography–United States.

All rights reserved. No part of this publication may be reproduced, stored in a retrieval system, or transmitted in any form or by any means—for example, electronic, photocopy, recording—without the prior written permission of the copyright owner.

All Scripture quotations, unless otherwise indicated, are taken from the Holy Bible, New International Version® (NIV). Copyright© 1973, 1978, 1984 by International Bible Society. Used by permission from Zondervan. All rights reserved.

Scripture quotations from The Message (MSG). Copyright© by Eugene H. Peterson 1993, 1994, 1995, 1996, 2000, 2001, 2002. Used by permission of NavPress Publishing Group.

Scripture taken from the New King James Version (NKJV). Copyright© 1982 by Thomas Nelson, Inc. Used by permission. All rights reserved.

Scripture quotations marked (CEV) are from the Contemporary English Version Copyright© 1991, 1992, 1995 by American Bible Society, used by permission.

Scripture quotations marked Revised Standard Version (RSV) of the Bible, copyright© 1946, 1952, and 1971 the Division of Christian Education of the National Council of the Churches of Christ in the United States of America. Used by permission. All rights reserved.

Scripture quotations marked (AMP) taken from the Amplified Bible Copyright© 1954, 1958, 1962, 1964, 1965, 1987 by The Lockman Foundation.

How Great Thou Art© 1949, 1953 The Stuart Hine Trust. All rights in the USA, its territories and possessions, except print rights, administered by Capitol CMG Publishing. USA, North, Central and South America print rights administered by Hope Publishing Company. All other non US Americas rights administered by The Stuart Hine Trust. Rest of world rights administered by Integrity Music UK. All rights reserved. Used by permission.

Vine's Expository Dictionary, W.E. Vine-Strong's Exhaustive Concordance (Vine's Dictionary)

Photography (including cover photo): Steve Lasher, www.LasherArts.com
Cover design: Lisa Vezina
Poems (unless noted otherwise): Teresa K. Lasher
Printed in the United States of America

In memory of my beloved mother,
Jimmie Joan Natalie Powders

February 1, 1932 – July 23, 1990

Dedicated to

To my dragon-slayer husband, Steve, who protected and lovingly nursed me back to health. His daily enduring love, faithfulness, and sacrifice does not go unnoticed. Through his eyes and the photography lens, he inspires the detection of beauty. My dearest children, Andrew (his wife Bethany) and Amanda; because of them, I embrace the title, Mom. My precious grandchildren: Liberty, Elijah, Ezekiel, and Ean; because of them, I proudly wear the title, Nana.

Acknowledgments

My heartfelt thanks to Word Weavers of West Michigan and Scribes writers' groups. You have provided much appreciated suggestions, critiquing, guidance, inspiration, and love in the bond of Christ. Reassuring words boosted my creative spirit infusing me with energy to keep on keeping on this rugged publication path.

Numerous conference presenters and facilitators along the way boosted my self-confidence and morale along this journey to completion.

A huge thank you to my editor, Kathy Bruins, to angel-helpers along the way, Dr. Jacqueline Rankin, Amanda Lasher, Chel Lasher, Kerry Kerr McAvoy, Jan Olexa, Noreen Ophoff, my amazing photographer-husband, Steve, cover designer Lisa Vezina, and others—you know who you are. My deepest gratitude to encouraging, supportive friends and family

Last, but not least, to my grace-filled, patient and loving Almighty God. With Him, all things are possible. I am a woman truly blessed who can honestly and wholeheartedly confess *Life is Good, Fragile, and Precious!*

Every good thing I have comes from You—Psalm 16:2/NLT.

Contents

Introduction 1

How do you rate according to the research? 4

Section 1   Mind (Life is Good) 7

    Chapter 1   Day 1-5   Time for Serious Introspection 9

    Chapter 2   Day 6-10   Courage vs. Cowardice 23

    Chapter 3   Day 11-15   Unplugged From the World 33

    Chapter 4   Day 16-20   Don't Worry About Tomorrow 45

    Chapter 5   Day 21-25   How Big is My God? 55

    Chapter 6   Day 26-30   Think on These Things 65

Section 2   Body (Life is Fragile) 77

    Chapter 7   Day 31-35   Escape and Enjoy Life! 79

    Chapter 8   Day 36-40   Fearfully and Wonderfully Made 93

    Chapter 9   Day 41-45   Strength to the Weary 103

    Chapter 10   Day 46-50   Years Fly Swiftly Away 113

    Chapter 11   Day 51-55   Had Your Nap Today? 125

    Chapter 12   Day 56-60   Slip Away 139

Section 3   Soul (Life is Precious) **153**

Chapter 13	Day 61-65	Solitary Place 155
Chapter 14	Day 66-70	All Other Ground is Sinking Sand 167
Chapter 15	Day 71-75	Faith and Nature Unite 179
Chapter 16	Day 76-80	Little Eyes Watch 191
Chapter 17	Day 81-85	Dress-up Time 205
Chapter 18	Day 86-90	Choose Joy 219

Parting Words 234

What gives you joy? 238

Special Song 242

Recipes 245

Good Reads 251

Connect with the Author 252

Endnotes.. 254

"What day is it?" asked Pooh.

"It's today," squeaked Piglet.

"My favorite day," said Pooh.[1]

"To live is the rarest thing in the world. Most people exist, that is all," Oscar Wilde.

Introduction

Discovery of a brain tumor triggered a realization that life was indeed *Good, Fragile, and Precious*. Picture *Runaway Bride* meets *While You Were Sleeping*. I am a brain surgery survivor and this is my grace story about a wake-up call which came in the form of a terrifying message from a doctor.

The Good News

- Survival and healing resulted
- I am not the same person as before the discovery of a tumor

A dear friend reminded me of a Scripture verse, quoted often but perhaps misunderstood: *Love your neighbor as yourself* (Mark 12:31). Further explanation revealed that in order to love others, I must first love myself. Those words caused me to realize that I loved others rather than myself. But that mindset would soon change. *Life is: Good, Fragile, and Precious* chronicles my journey of what happened and the lessons learned from the ordeal.

Glimpses of 90 days of this frightening health crisis are taken from my personal journal entries. I share interactive tips on fighting a battle to regain control over proper care of three areas of life—mind, body, and soul; the foundation for loving one's self. Only then could I walk the path toward healing and restoration. When one aspect is suffering or out of balance, the rest of our being suffers. A quotation from Joan Anderson echoes my own journey, "My job was to save the only life I could save—my own! … She showed me how to dance beyond the breakers, to pick up the dropped stitches of my life, to live in the moment, to nourish and love my body, and to never stop embracing adventure."[2] *Life is: Good, Fragile, and Precious* is for anyone on a quest to live a balanced, fulfilled life.

- **Life can be truly good (Mind):** understanding, moral reflection, imagination, or meditation (*Vine's Dictionary*). We will explore creative suggestions for setting aside fears and worries allowing God control of your mind. No matter the circumstances, let go and let God.

- **Life is fragile (Body)**: tomorrow is not promised. The only moment that is promised to us is this exact moment. Thank God for your wonderful aging and changing body (bruises, scars and all). He woke you up this morning, didn't He? If you are reading these words, it is not too late to begin caring for your body, God's temple. *Life is: Good, Fragile, and Precious* takes a look at ways to appreciate and care for your changing body.

- **Life is precious (Spiritual Health/Soul):** the breath of life, will and purpose, seat of personality, the emotional element by which he perceives, reflects, feel and desires (*Vine's Dictionary*). Being still for a portion of the day allows re-energization resulting in joy and peace. How does one go about doing that in the midst of crazy-busy days?

Readers of all ages will discover wealth in the humor, enriching stories and quotes. In addition to each focused theme, I include five supplemental days of related anecdotes. After each day's meditation/devotion, interactive questions and reflective thoughts follow. The sections are short and sweet allowing time to absorb a morsel of truth before work or class, during a lunch break, or before nodding off to sleep.

Treat yourself to a new journal, grab a favorite writing instrument and join this brain surgery survivor in rediscovering yourself and the preciousness of life. As you read these words from a fellow traveler, I pray you will see **less** of me and the ordeal of brain surgery, and **more** of the secure, immovable Rock—God, the Father. Live in and enjoy this present moment ... God's remarkable gift to you right here and now.

> *God so loved the world that he gave his one and only Son, that whoever believes in him shall not perish but have eternal life—*
> Life-giving words from John 3:16.

Blessings from a fellow pilgrim,

Teresa K. Lasher

How do you rate according to the research?

Loving ourselves implies we take care of our body by eating properly, exercising regularly, monitoring our hours at work, and getting the proper amount of sleep and quiet time. Most of us know these truths, but they are hard to put into practice in today's culture. The question is: Do we act upon what we know to be true?

Americans tend to work and eat more, and at the same time, sleep and play less. Consequently, our solitude time shrinks. Yet we wonder why our effectiveness and quality of life decrease. There was enough evidence for me to stand guilty on all counts of not caring for my body. According to statistics, I am not alone.

Studies from Families and Work Institute, National Study of the Changing Workforce (NSCW):

- 59% of employees report not having enough time for themselves
- 61% report not having enough time to spend with their partners or spouses
- 75% report not having enough time to spend with their children
- Only 28% of employees today report that their overall health is "excellent," down from 34% just six years ago
- Nearly half of U.S. employees (49%) have not engaged in regular physical exercise in the past 30 days
- 58% of American adults complain of insomnia. Sleep specialists and scientists know that adequate sleep is necessary for healthy functioning, regulates mood, and is related to learning and memory functions. Sleep contributes to wellness as does exercise and nutrition (National Sleep Foundation)

Families and Work Institute reports that Americans do not take adequate time to care for their bodies, "in the midst of the most vigorous national health-care debate in 15 years, and at a time of heightened economic insecurity, new data shows that the health of employed American workers is trending downward in a number of important areas."[3]

When the above lifestyle issues continue this out-of-balance trend, signs of discontent and failing health may result. A great percentage of women are employed outside the home. Then they come home to their second or third job in the home feeling exhausted with little time or energy to care for themselves. Parenting, regardless of the children's ages, takes hours of care oftentimes leaving parents emotionally and physically drained.

- 68 million women work in the civilian labor force
- 63% of women work outside the home
- 54% of women work full-time
- 77% of all mothers with school age children (6-17) work according to data compiled on: www.womenemployed.org.

Many people become primary caregivers to others in their spheres of influence. Since approximately 49% of the U.S. adult population shoulder elder care responsibilities, this can lead to neglect of their own bodies. Friends in our sphere of influence shoulder additional responsibilities such as caring for elderly parents (part time or sole responsibility), grandchildren or siblings. These often necessary added burdens weigh heavily on a day-to-day basis. This is when even more conscious, deliberate me-time is needed. Unfortunately, due to time constraints, me-time gets pushed further and further away.

As you read this ninety-day meditation and devotional journey, the author desires healing and restoration of your mind, body, and soul. Readers of all ages will find benefit in the practical guidance, insights, and wisdom shared from a desperate place of knowing change was needed. With that change came benefits of healing and wholeness. Watch as you witness your crazy-busy lifestyle turn into a much healthier life!

Section 1

Mind (Life is Good)

Chapter 1

Time for Serious Introspection

Trust in the Lord with all your heart and lean not on your own understanding; in all your ways acknowledge him, and he will make your paths straight—Proverbs 3:5–6.

"Hello, this is the doctor's office. We have the results from your MRI. As soon as you receive this message, please return the call."

The voicemail immediately captured my attention. *Who is calling so early? This cannot be real—I must be hearing things.* I rolled over and plopped a pillow over my head. My mind spun in a one thousand different directions; my heart beat faster. After a few minutes of pretending I was dreaming, I could not contain my curiosity any longer. Feeling as though I carried a backpack full of a semester's worth of books, I walked to the source of the ominous message. After replaying the message several times, I called the office back. A morning appointment had already been scheduled for me with no further details. This could not be good news. No one bothered to ask if I had other plans for the day.

On the ride to my doctor's office, I don't remember what words were exchanged between my husband Steve and me. Random, irrational thoughts bombarded my head. *Would I live to see my daughter marry? Create sandcastles with our grandchildren? Retire and travel to exotic places with my hubby?* The scary "c" word immediately popped into my mind, but until we talked with the doctor, I wouldn't know if cancer posed a possibility. All the way there, words between us remained few other than my muttering several times, *Why couldn't this wait till next week or next month, or never?*

My family doctor described the preliminary MRI[4] findings by showing us images of my brain. He wanted us to talk more in depth with a neurosurgeon that same day. So that afternoon, Steve and I sat in an unfamiliar office where a specialist explained more about the tumor and discussed my MRI scan which glared at us from a computer screen. He explained that a large tumor rested near my optic nerve along the left side of my brain. He used the word *meningioma*[5] in my left temporal tip. Extensive test results revealed a partial peripheral deterioration in my left eye. Surgery was recommended in order to minimize any further weakening of the eye. This tumor was likely benign. I wanted to know how the tumor got there and how long it had been growing. The surgeon's only response was that the tumor needed attention. If left unchecked, it could adversely affect my vision and other areas. An issue of life or death was not what I'd planned for the upcoming holiday weekend.

The neurosurgeon exhibited a quiet gentleness. We learned later that he came in on his day off to share this news with us. After further research, I discovered that he previously practiced in Boston. Just months prior to my diagnosis our local hospital had recruited him. Before that time, there had not been a neurosurgeon in town experienced in this type of surgery. I call this coincidence a God-thing. Even before I knew of this specific need, God had the task covered. Having the surgery done locally and not needing to travel out of state for extensive surgery granted us a measure of peace. Recovery could take place near home—close to my supportive family and friends.

I immediately sent an SOS request to family members and friends asking for prayers. This journey could not be taken in my strength alone.

- In what ways are you obedient to His Word? Are there ways you pretend to be obedient? If changes need to be made, what concerns do you have if/when this change takes place?
- What in your life IS pleasing to God? Is there something gnawing away at you that is not pleasing to Him? Are there changes that need to be addressed? List them below or in your journal.
- How can you model trust for others to see? Folks would ask what church Steve's grandfather attended. I love his classic response, "I'm a follower of the Lord Jesus Christ." He got right down to the core truth of a believer's life. Is there sufficient evidence in your life for this kind of trust?

Prayer of Encouragement:

    I realize the need to simplify my life. I give up trying to figure things out on my own. Instead, I leave the whole simplifying-my-life-process, medical outcome, financial, and other troubles in Your capable, trustworthy hands. Amen.

Day 1

Those who trust in the Lord are like Mount Zion, which cannot be shaken but endures forever. As the mountains surround Jerusalem, so the Lord surrounds his people both now and forevermore—Psalm 125:1–2.

One friend did not hesitate to share his views on my dilemma. Knowing I was in turmoil, he approached me saying,

"Teresa, I have a verse for you."

"Okay, Bob, what is it?"

"Love your neighbor as yourself."

"Sure, I've heard that Bible verse. But what does it have to do with me right now?"

He explained that the verse does not say to love our neighbors *more* than ourselves. So it is reasonable to conclude that since we are to love our neighbors as *much* as we love ourselves, it's obvious that we are to love ourselves. How would I even begin to apply those five simple words to everyday life? The majority of my life I perceived others as more significant and deserving than me.

In Jesus' day, Jewish religious leaders questioned Jesus,

Of all the commandments, which is the most important? The most important one, answered Jesus, is this: Love the Lord your God with all your heart and with all your soul and with all your mind and with all your strength. The second is this: Love your neighbor as yourself. There is no commandment greater than these (Mark 12:28–31).
Jesus added, Do this and you will live (Luke 10:28).

It was a revolutionary idea then and still is today. Even though the idea made sense, the implementation proved more challenging. Bob and his wife, Vicki, were kind enough to brainstorm with Steve and me to help discern what loving myself might look like. Leaving my stressful job appeared at the top of the discussion list. This choice also freed me to follow my passion for writing. Focusing on becoming a happier, healthier self would be my prime directive. I didn't realize how life-changing that verse would be in the following days and months.

At the onset of this new revelation, I knew the challenge to become stress-free and unclutter my life would be a tough (and sometimes unpopular) assignment. To take care of my own body, it was necessary to reduce distractions and strive to live out the command, *Be still, and know that I am God* (Psalm 46:10). Routinely, I scheduled my life with busyness not giving much thought about short or long-term goals. If I worked on the loving my neighbor as myself concept, I knew now was the time to get my life (mind, body, and soul) in order.

I started asking myself questions, *What things or people in my life create undue stress? Who do I need to visit, call, or write? What projects need completion and which ones can wait?* My responsibility was to place myself in the healthiest position possible in preparation for surgery and subsequent recovery.

Then we played the waiting game. Waiting for the right doctors to be found and asked to perform the surgery. Waiting for a physician to return from vacation. After all the players lined up, the surgery date could be set. My outlook on life changed after viewing the MRI revealing a brain tumor. Minor details, such as a sticky spot on the kitchen counter or scheduling a hair appointment, did not seem to matter anymore. Now my world revolved around researching this type of brain tumor and the best doctors to perform the surgery. To move forward, I needed to resist dwelling on partial peripheral vision loss or the possible negative results of major surgery.

Day 1-5   *Time for Serious Introspection*

    Heavy stress accompanied me day after day. When I was at work, my mind thought about unfinished projects waiting at home; while at home, my mind thought about work. Unexplainable emptiness and lack of focus pervaded my being. Something was out of sync in my life, but what was it? I could not go on living in this state of unrest. It was time to take an honest inventory of my life to determine exactly what I faced:

- a life-threatening health issue
- employment at a job I disliked
- lack of balance and wellness in my mind, body, and soul

    It's easy to say that I trust God when life flows smoothly. However, the forecast warned of stormy weather and rough seas ahead. I felt privileged to be surrounded by a loving, supportive husband, family and friends. After brainstorming and praying with my support staff, I knew what would be my first step.

    I paused to hum these words to *Leaning on the Everlasting Arms* and allow their meaning to permeate deep within my soul.

Leaning On the Everlasting Arms

What have I to dread, what have I to fear,

Leaning on the everlasting arms?

I have blessed peace with my Lord so near,

Leaning on the everlasting arms.

Leaning, leaning,

Safe and secure from all alarms;

Leaning, leaning,

Leaning on the everlasting arms.[6]

- What or whom do you depend on? Will it/they falter and change like shifting sand? Make notes in your journal.
- What part of your life haven't you released to God in trust? Why? Take some time and formulate a prayer to God regarding this.
- Would others see your faith? Would your faith resemble sinking sand, or a mountain, dependable and unmovable? Give an example.

Day 2

For I am the LORD, your God, who takes hold of your right hand and says to you, Do not fear; I will help you—Isaiah 41:13.

Nearby, God is waiting and wanting me to reach out and trust Him. He will guide me through the stormy waters and past the deep pits in my life; I need never walk alone. I firmly believe God is in this. He knows all about my brain tumor. I continually remind myself to trust Him and His infinite wisdom. He loves me and always has my best interests in mind. Even when I cannot see the beginning from the end—He sees the whole big picture.

Our former senior pastor, Ed Dobson, wrote a book called *Prayers & Promises when facing a life-threatening illness.* [7] He tells of his tough decision to step down as pastor of a large church after discovering he had a progressive life-threatening disease, ALS.[8] Pastor Ed discovered God's grace was sufficient. He urged the reader to learn to pray, "God, give me the grace to let go of my job. And give me the grace to see my identity as more than what I do."

I can relate to those words. A job or specific position is not entirely who we are. Our being is comprised of more than our career. I sensed that working at my current job, with its accompanying stress and unfulfilled promises, was no longer what God desired for me. Continuing work at this location violated the issue of properly taking care of myself. The mere thought of leaving lifted my spirits. If I quit, then I could attend to my body and prepare for surgery and subsequent recovery. This decision would also allow more time to use my God-given passion to write and tell others of God's faithfulness and answers to prayer. A smile crept over my face.

"Trust God today no matter how dark your situation. God says 'You are coming out!' When a train goes through a tunnel and it gets dark, you don't throw away the ticket and jump off. You sit still and trust the engineer,"
Corrie Ten Boom.

- Write down your fears and doubts of today. God is listening. His shoulders are big enough to handle anything you experience.
- How has God proven His faithfulness in the past? Record those special times and circumstances in your journal.
- What prevents you from trusting Him with your cares now?

Day 3

The LORD himself goes before you and will be with you; he will never leave you nor forsake you. Do not be afraid; do not be discouraged—Deuteronomy 31:8.

There are no guarantees for a happy or healthy life. However, this passage gives me confidence to know that when I place my trust in God, I have the assurance He will not abandon me in the middle of a crisis or afterwards. Just knowing He is there beside me each step of the way causes my mind and heart to feel at peace.

The ability to focus becomes increasingly harder to accomplish. I feel jittery, tense, wanting to be someplace else. Prior to the surgery date, I need to tell my manager that I plan to quit. I don't want sympathy, just prayer and encouragement. I'm essentially the same person as before the tumor diagnosis. Needing some me-time, I travel to the water and pen these words:

> I go to my Sanctuary
> Quiet reigns
> Except for quacking geese
> Nearby culinary smells of
> Freshly baked bread

Day 1-5   Time for Serious Introspection

American flag flutters over stern
A solitary sailboat with jib hoisted
Moves slowly across the lake

Peace prevails without
From within, my spirit begins to calm

Sun's set
Cloud bank lines horizon
Rained last 24 hours
Only the valiant
Brave the outdoors tonight
Prepare for war
Prepare to serve
Be a shining light

All is calm
All is well with my soul

"When you get into a tight place and everything goes against you, till it seems as though you could not hang on a minute longer, never give up then, for that is just the place and time that the tide will turn,"
Harriet Beecher Stowe.

- Have you ever felt unable to focus because of anxiety and worry? What is it like for you?
- Do you fear your spouse, family member, or friends might desert you if you would become sick or hospitalized?
- What are you feeling discouraged about? Record those nagging thoughts in your journal.

Day 4

O God, thou art my God; early will I seek thee: my soul thirsteth for thee, my flesh longeth for thee in a dry and thirsty land, where no water is; to see thy power and thy glory, so as I have seen thee in the sanctuary—Psalm 63:1–2 (KJV).

The medical facility I visited for my MRI exam was amazing, new, and bright. The designer understood the importance of light and foliage to uplift soul and spirit. After my procedure in the MRI cocoon with jack hammer sounds in my head and ears, I was ready for some quiet time. I took the elevator to the top of the building following a sign that read, Meditation Room. Windows surround the entire circular space. Comfortable chairs and sofas are positioned in perfect view of the entire downtown business area. My first reaction: WOW! Immediately I felt the warmth of the sun wrapping long arms around my shoulders. Almost as if to say, "It's going to be all right."

I noticed several inspirational literature pieces on the window ledge. A prayer card caught my eye as I settled into a chair and read the following:

Day 1-5   *Time for Serious Introspection*

> LORD, help me to remember that nothing is going to happen to me today that You and I together can't handle.

You, God, are my God, earnestly I seek you; I thirst for you, my whole being longs for you, in a dry and parched land where there is no water. I have seen you in the sanctuary and beheld your power and your glory. Because your love is better than life, my lips will glorify you. I will praise you as long as I live, and in your name I will lift up my hands—Psalm 63:1-4.

- In what circumstance do you find yourself seeking other people's affirmation or approval? Name that circumstance in your journal.
- Is there anything or anyone you value above God? Research and consider the word idol.
- When is your best time to soak in Scripture verses and talk to God uninterrupted? Your best time more than likely will vary from other family members. He longs to hear from you anytime day or night.

Day 5

For I know the plans I have for you, declares the Lord, plans to prosper you and not to harm you, plans to give you hope and a future. Then you will call upon me and come and pray to me, and I will listen to you. You will seek me and find me when you seek me with all your heart, I will be found by you, declares the Lord, and will bring you back from captivity— Jeremiah 29:11–13.

As a young mom, I remember the first time I heard an airplane stewardess explain the proper use of an oxygen mask. Since I'd never flown before, I listened intently wanting to be sure I knew exactly what to do in the event of a plane crash. She instructed us to first place the mask over our own face and mouth prior to helping a child or an elderly person. After a mask was securely fastened to our face, then we should place the mask over the child's face. *Put my own mask on first? Did I hear her correctly? Isn't that selfish not placing my child's wellbeing into consideration first?* As I pondered the instructions, it dawned on me that if I did not take proper care of attending to my own oxygen needs, I would not be alive to help a dependent child or elderly person in an adjacent seat. The same guidelines apply here. My task is to attend to my basic needs so that I'll be available to help others in need. So it is with life.

I see the correlation between taking care of my body, mind, and soul. When I do this, I'm able to witness and enjoy my children, grandchildren, and family grow older and prosper. It makes sense to take care of our bodies in order to be alive, fit, and available for others. If you do not take care of you, then who will? Taking care of you is not a selfish endeavor, but a wise and necessary one. The apostle Paul says, *After all, no one ever hated their own body, but they feed and care for their body, just as Christ does the church—for we are members of his body* (Ephesians 5:29–30).

Today is the day I tell my co-workers that I'm giving notice to quit. God gives us Christian friends here on earth to model Jesus. I found it interesting the various reactions received after they learned of my intention:

"How awful! I am so sorry."

"If you leave now, you'll be putting us in a difficult position to try and replace you."

"Good thing they found out early before it affected your vision anymore and other vital parts."

Day 1-5   *Time for Serious Introspection*

A few patted me on the shoulder; others hugged me. Now I did not have to hide behind a host of appointments. The word is out in the open. Being free and honest is my preference. Somehow, this surgery all plays into my future. What or how? I do not know, but He does.

Jewish commentator, Rabbi Hirsch, interprets Psalm 23:1 this way: "The Lord is my shepherd therefore I suffer no want. I do not miss what I do not have. I do not feel its lack, since it is God, my shepherd, who had seen fit to withhold it from me. He shows me His love by denying me that which I desire, but which if I was to have, it would cause me harm."

- What do you long for more than anything else?
- Have you prayed asking God for wisdom about your longing? Write out your prayer in your journal.
- If you believe God has your best interests in mind, how and what should you pray?

Prayer of Encouragement:

Father God, I step aside and give You full reign in my life regardless of the outcome. My soul yearns for fulfillment, my flesh longs for You—for completeness, wholeness, satisfaction. Your intent is not to harm. Why do I wander to other sources when only You can fill me? I need to look no further for someone or something else to fill that empty spot. I cling to You for dear life because You are my steady rock.

I invite you to reflect on benefits of Godly wisdom found in Proverbs 3.

Chapter 2

Courage vs. Cowardice

Brain surgery! Seriously? That is not a routine procedure. At least not in my circle of family and friends. Conflict rages inside me. I am afraid, nervous, and feel totally out of control. I was in shock. The diagnosis must be a mistake. This is a cruel joke or maybe I'm dreaming. But it is real ... and it's a nightmare from which I desperately want to wake up. Maybe if I pretend to go about my normal life, this will just go away.

Sadly, I was wide awake and could not get away from reality. At times, I felt at peace knowing God remained in control. Other times, I wanted to run in the opposite direction. An eight-hour surgery was what the specialist predicted, with a week's hospital stay and follow-up rehabilitation. This multifaceted operation would be done by a team of doctors including a neurosurgeon who would remove the tumor and a plastic surgeon to realign and reattach the affected areas from the top of my scalp back across my head and around to the front of my ear.

Before surgery day, my husband and I attended a worship service where our pastor spoke about David, the shepherd boy. David battled an enemy, a giant named Goliath. While preparing for battle, refusing King Saul's coat of armor and helmet; instead choosing five smooth stones from a stream. A peculiar choice to me; yet he spoke boldly to the giant. *You come against me with sword and spear and javelin, but I come against you in the name of the Lord Almighty ... and the whole world will know that there is a God ... the battle is the Lord's* (1 Samuel 17:45–47).

David proved to be a brave man of action. He did not allow Goliath's colossal bulk to thwart his determination to win the battle. The giant's size alone could have been overwhelming to David, causing him to feel helpless and forget the mighty power of God. His family and friends taunted him, yet David moved forward into battle and killed Goliath. His tremendous courage and reliance on his great God brought victory—through the use of one small stone.

My giant was spelled F-E-A-R! I could not allow this raging torment of anxiety to consume my thoughts and rule my mind, body, and soul. If anxiety controlled, defeat would come before the healing process even began. Circumstances appeared bleak and scary, but I need to remember that God is bigger than any challenge. Like David, when I seek God's strength in my life, I experience His supernatural power. Paralyzing fear of the future does not need to overwhelm me. Leaning on God and allowing Him to shoulder my concerns and doubts is my choice. As I look death straight in the eye, I say, *The battle is the Lord's.*

- When do you feel fearful or overwhelmed by life? List those critical times.
- What do you worry about? Maybe one of your children, family or friend relationships, fear of job loss, or home foreclosure? Be specific.
- Are you fearful to the point of being immobilized and unable to cope with life's smallest choices?
- If fear is a huge part of your life, how might you turn that around to the positive? Consider keeping a separate grateful list in your journal.

Prayer of Encouragement:

Lord, I choose to place my faith in You and in Your power. You are mightier than any fear in my life. Flood my heart with Your grace and peace. Replace my cowardice with courage, so that I can overcome giants. May others see this hope within me and be encouraged. I thank You in advance for victory. Amen.

Day 6

The Lord is my light and my salvation—whom shall I fear? The Lord is the stronghold of my life—of whom shall I be afraid?—Psalm 27:1.

I awaken early with my mind discombobulated. Anxious, sometimes fearful thoughts, pop into my head. *What's my next step? Do they plan to remove the entire tumor? Can I find out the doctor's success rate? What are the risks involved in this type of surgery?*

God is so good. He orchestrated our time with friends over breakfast. They listened to my heart cry and spoke words of wisdom originating from the Bible. Gentle advice shared at just the right time. Psalm 27 states that God is my light. If He is my light, then I need not fear the dark. God is bigger than any fear I experience today. I need to honestly tell God my fears; He won't be surprised. God longs for me to share my burdens. I do not know what tomorrow holds, but God does. I can trust Him fully in all things and situations.

I spy a sliver of the moon this morning. Only a tiny glimpse. He reveals another piece of His character when I walk through my day in faith. Not a lot of light, just enough to see the next few steps ahead. God is always on time.

Day 6-10   *Courage vs. Cowardice*

- What or whom do you turn to in times of trouble?
- Confess any fear(s) and doubt(s) to God in prayer.
- Whom can you trust and confide in to pray with you? What characteristic(s) do they have that makes you trust them?

Day 7

For in the day of trouble, he will keep me safe in his dwelling; he will hide me in the shelter of his tabernacle and set me high upon a rock—Psalm 27:5.

The summer before my surgery, Bonnie, a long-time friend from Pennsylvania, traveled to Michigan to assist with my niece's high school graduation party. We've been friends since B.K. (before kids). During a walk together, she asked a question.

"Teresa, I noticed your left eye seems swollen. Have you had it checked?"

I was surprised at the question. The swelling happened so gradually that I had not thought much about it, and I said, "No, I'm just living with it and assumed the puffiness was due to allergies or lack of sleep."

"I think it might be a good idea to have it checked out anyway. It could be nothing, or it could be something," Bonnie said.

I was frustrated with my left eye even to the point of asking another friend to help me cover the affected area with makeup. Additional makeup did not really do any good, so I continued to blame allergies or just the fact of getting older. I know God hides me in His shelter when I confess my troubles to Him. As I name my trouble, I release my burden to God and refuse to take it back.

- Do you feel as though you are in the day of trouble right now? Name the trouble.
- Pray and shift the burden over to an all-knowing Creator. Express those concerns to God, pray, asking Him to help you release them.
- How do you know God is protecting you?
- What evidence have you felt/seen of God's protection?

Day 8

Hear my voice when I call, O LORD; be merciful to me and answer me—Psalm 27:7.

Psalm 27 tells me that God hears my pleas of doubt, fear, and desperation. He will answer and forgive me my wrong choices—one of them being worry. I choose to call upon the name of the Lord and ask for forgiveness. *I am so thankful, God, that You are merciful to forgive. You have the ability to wash me whiter than snow.*

This time, because of my friend's concern and comment about my eye, I took her advice and made an appointment with my internist. Part of the reason no one else noticed my swollen eye was because they saw me all the time and did not notice the gradual change in my facial symmetry.

A friend confides that he awoke at 3 a.m., thought of me right away and prayed. To hear this confirms to me that God is at work behind the scenes. I continue to receive notes, cards, and phone calls affirming peoples' love and concerns.

Did I plan to have brain surgery? Of course not. But the almighty Creator of the universe, and Creator of me, knew this time would come. Worry or fear will not change the outcome of this story. Trusting in God can make a difference in my perspective and how others view my problem. I need to decide if I will call upon God when my world seems to be crumbling. Others watch as I act and react. Will my actions match my words and proclaimed faith?

> "Overthinking: the art of creating problems that weren't even there," Unknown.

- Do you find it awkward to call on God's name? If so, why? If not, what has helped you trust God?
- Is there something in your life of which you are not proud? Although God knows about it, write it out for your own release. This method can be therapeutic.
- Sit in God's presence. Be still and listen to Him. What do you hear?

Day 9

My heart says of you, Seek his face! Your face, LORD, I will seek. Do not hide your face from me, do not turn your servant away in anger; you have been my helper. Do not reject me or forsake me, O God my Savior—Psalm 27:8–9.

Today was a good day. I received positive affirmation from my Aquinas College writers' group about this story. My profitable time in group made the day sail by. After sharing my work-in-progress, they shared ideas on different avenues and publications to research. Overall, they felt the story was impactful and would hold interest to a variety of people. Several took me aside saying they would be my prayer warrior. Someone to fight this battle with me in prayer.

Forgive me, God, for not trusting. You are enough to handle my problems. Do not hide Your face from me now. I need You now more than ever. I must be calm and assured. I have Your word that promises to walk with me through the storm.

- In what way do you act as though God is your Helper? In what circumstance are you more likely to push through in your own strength, or call on God's help?
- When was the last time you turned to Him in time of trouble? What happened?
- Is God your Savior? If so, thank Him. If not, pause and ask Him to be your Savior.

Day 10

I am still confident of this: I will see the goodness of the LORD in the land of the living. Wait for the LORD; be strong and take heart and wait for the LORD—
Psalm 27:13–14.

My family doctor immediately ordered a complete blood workup. He suggested I make an extensive eye exam appointment with an ophthalmologist, and schedule an MRI. My blood work showed nothing to be alarmed about. My left eye tested slightly worse than last year; right eye seemed improved. The eye doctor found nothing out of the ordinary.

When it came to making an appointment for the MRI, I resisted. I made an appointment, but cancelled and rescheduled not wanting to undergo all the time and money involved. I reasoned they probably wouldn't find anything anyway. Thankfully, my internist hounded me at my next routine appointment.

"So, did you have an MRI yet?" asked my doctor.

"I did schedule it, but had to cancel. I thought maybe we could just skip the MRI," I said hoping he would drop the subject and move on to other topics.

"Oh no, I think you should get one to see if we can figure out what is going on with your left eye. In fact, I feel the eye doctor dropped the ball when he didn't push for an MRI."

My avoidance tactic didn't work.

In order to appease my doctor, I rescheduled my MRI appointment. And this time, I kept the appointment.

- When was the last time you went ahead of God and did your own thing? Is there something you know God wants you to do but you might be avoiding?
- Think about the outcome of that decision.
- What results have you noticed when you wait on God, His answers, and instructions?

Prayer of Encouragement:

Lord, I've done my own thing for too long. To be honest, most of the time it did not work out. I run ahead of You trying to figure out a possible resolution using my own wisdom. I'm ready to be led by You, willing to be molded, and used as You see fit. Amen.

I invite you to read and reflect on the healing, hopeful words found in Psalm 27.

Day 6-10   Courage vs. Cowardice

Chapter 3

Unplugged From the World

At daybreak Jesus went out to a solitary place—Luke 4:42.

Once during a meeting, I jumped out of my comfortable chair to retrieve my cell phone I forgot in my car. I trudged down two flights of stairs, through the entire length of the building and out into the pouring rain. There was a time I fought to avoid carrying a cell phone thinking, *This device is like an electronic tether monitoring my every move. What next, will it critique my motivation and mood? What has my life come to? Am I guilty of being selfish for not wanting to be connected constantly? Is it a criminal offense to desire to be unplugged for 15 minutes, an hour or maybe even a day? I'm not even expecting an important call.*

There is a time and a place to be quiet. Jesus understood the proper equilibrium. He purposely walked to a deserted place away from exhausting throngs of people. Spending time with His Father, He sought solitude for prayer and refreshment. Jesus had command of legions of angels and the entire universe, yet he demonstrated the importance of unplugging in order to minister more fully and completely to others. If Jesus felt the necessity to distance Himself from the pressing of people for a period of time, it is even more critical for me to do the same.

Jesus understood boundaries. We need boundaries in several areas including vocational, relational, and emotional. Read along and follow these next few verses and see if you agree. Do you get a sense of His determination and mission? He never lost sight of the goal.

Early the next morning Jesus went out to an isolated place. The crowds searched everywhere for him, and when they finally found him, they begged him not to leave them. But he replied, I must preach the Good News of the Kingdom of God in other towns, too, because that is why I was sent. So he continued to travel around, preaching in synagogues throughout Judea— Luke 4:42–44/NLT.

You can't DO everything! There is what you **could** do. There is what others believe you **should** do. Priorities are the things you **must** do. Here is an example shared by Pastor Craig:[9]

1. I must spend time with God. No one else can do this for me.
2. I must date my spouse.
3. I must invest in my children, grandchildren, and great-grandchildren (if you have any).

Remember these three D's:

1. **Disconnect** to connect with those we love
2. **Deepen** our value of reality
3. **Develop** clear, healthy boundaries

- How much time do you spend glued to electronic devices? If you feel the need to reduce that time, what is your plan to accomplish this?
- How well are you doing with the priorities listed above? What excuse (if any) do you use for not spending time alone with God and your loved ones?
- How well are you doing on boundary setting? If Jesus felt the need to step aside, when will you make this a priority in your life (if you haven't already)?

Prayer of Encouragement:

Forgive me, God, for wanting to constantly **do**. Help me find that quiet, solitude time to just **be** in Your presence. I want to be more excited about growing close to You than I am about knowing what is going on around me. Knowing this is a huge request, thank you for being faithful when I am not. Amen.

Day 11

"When we have met our Lord in the silent intimacy of our prayer, then we will also meet Him ... in the market, and in the town square. But when we have not met Him in the center of our own hearts, we cannot expect to meet Him in the busyness of our daily lives," Henri Nouwen.

Days after finding out about the tumor, I rise early that morning. My mind wanders to a thought, *what if these really were my last days, knowing that all my days are numbered.* Thinking about mortality forces me to think seriously. This is not just another ordinary day. It is a brand new day. A chance to right wrongs. To live life fully and in the present. Yet, aren't we to live every day as if it might be our last one here on earth? I certainly do not function that way most of the time.

Then I hear the rain. I venture out onto my deck. Blessed rain. We need the rain on the dry spaces. Thank God for rain. Reminds me of new life. A fresh start.

I did not miss being unplugged at all. It was a good start to a new me. When I take the time early in the morning to pause and thank my Heavenly Father for His abundant blessings, my day goes smoother. I need to go to Him before I face anyone else. Unfortunately, all too often, I struggle through the day in my own strength. Those are usually the days I grow to regret part of my day. Do I detect kindred spirit here?

- What devotional (some suggestions are in back of this book), along with a Bible passage/verse, could you meditate on to help your pilgrim-traveller journey? Verse prompts: Psalm 111 (holy and awesome God, He has done great works); Matthew 11:28 (go to God you who are weary, and He will give you rest); Matthew 14:27 (do not be afraid); Hebrews 13:5-8 (I will never leave you, nor forsake you).
- What concern presses in on your heart? Can you share it with God?
- How was your whole heart involved when you communicated with God? What does the term whole heart mean to you? (Suggestions to jump start your thought processes: complete, total, undivided attention.)

Day 12

Be still, and know that I am God … The Lord Almighty is with us; the God of Jacob is our fortress—Psalm 46:10–11.

Be still, and know that I am God. Only eight words, but not so simple to execute. Be still means to cease striving. Quit trying to figure and wiggle out of a situation or problem. Allow God's timing to remedy and mature. Again, much easier said than done in this age of want-it-my-way within my timeframe.

During the weeks leading up to surgery, I am amazed at how music, certain words to a song, or the pastor's message speaks to my heart and soul. Worship takes heart preparation time. Rushing in the midst of multiple distractions defeats the purpose of quieting one's heart.

I love how the Amplified Bible explains those two verses in Psalm 46 a bit deeper. *Let be and be still, and know* (recognize and understand) *that I am God.*

Day 11-15   Unplugged From the World

I will be exalted among the nations! I will be exalted in the earth! The Lord of hosts is with us; the God of Jacob is our Refuge (our High Tower and Stronghold). *Selah* [pause, and calmly think of that]!

We, as human beings, will never be able to fully understand God's doings or reasoning. But we are capable of acknowledging the God of the universe and trying to please Him in every way we know possible. We can pause and think calmly of all He is and has done for us. When the wind blows briskly, thunder booms, lightening crackles, and rain pours in torrents, we can be assured He knows. He cares. Safe and secure in my heavenly Father's arms as I run right back to my High Tower.

My mind zooms ahead to what I need to pack for my hospital stay. A robe when I am able to eventually roam the halls, make-up—never mind, no amount of make-up will cover the marks left behind. I planned and fretted about which suitcase to take with me. Now I realize how silly all that planning and fretting sounds.

In reality, just a few essential basics are all I really need: faith, hope, and love. Guess what? Those items do not require a suitcase. I carry them in my head and in my heart. Faith in my God to see me through. Hope and love shown to me by my stick-by-me spouse, daughter, son and wife, plus others. So thankful for faithful prayer warriors who pray me through, shower me with words of encouragement, gifts, and positive thoughts.

Therefore, we do not lose heart. Though outwardly we are wasting away, yet inwardly we are being renewed day by day. For our light and momentary troubles are achieving for us an eternal glory that far outweighs them all. So we fix our eyes not on what is seen, but on what is unseen, since what is seen is temporary, but what is unseen is eternal—
2 Corinthians 4:16–18.

- How well did you follow the instructions in Psalm 46:10 before rushing out the door or attend to business at home? If you did not score well, remember tomorrow is another day to aim for success.
- Where can you go to escape normal routines and concentrate fully on God? What do you normally do there? Secret: distractedness is a problem for me. I am still a work-in-progress.
- What is your plan to spend more time with God? Do you need to rise earlier, or stay up later to capture that sacred time? What works personally for you and why?

Day 13

Blessed is the one … whose delight is in the law of the Lord, and who meditates on his law day and night. That person is like a tree planted by streams of water, which yields its fruit in season and whose leaf does not wither—whatever they do prospers—Psalm 1:1–4.

I awake startled, unsettled, and crying. My dream: two fighting cats: one large and one small. The small cat lost her entire eye in a fight. She looked ugly. I felt no one would want or love her ever again. *Will I lose my eye or eyesight? After surgery, will I look the same or behave differently? What about others; will they feel the same about me?*

Not only do I come to God for refreshment, but He delights in the fact that I *choose* to come to Him. I desire that connectedness. I can catch up with people later. Being unplugged from electronic devices and plugged into God is priceless. Meditation is not a one-time task. It's a repeat practice … again and again. Daily, I desire God's wisdom and strength. Am I willing to seek after that goal; are you?

Day 11-15 Unplugged From the World

My hubby suggested we take a final cruise on our sailboat for the season. When living in the Midwest, boaters prep their boats for haul out and winter storage. Wind fills our jib[10] while we keep company with a speckling of other die-hard sailors. Beautiful, glorious final sail. As we depart the marina, we say good-bye and "see ya in the spring" to our fellow comrades. On to the next season and chapter of life's journey. We soaked up as much sun as possible trying to bank ahead a reserve of vitamin D knowing long, dreary winter months loom ahead. Thoughts gleaned from Psalm 25:

> No one whose hope is in You
> Will ever be put to shame
> Only those who are treacherous
> Without excuse
>
> Show me Your ways
> Teach me Your paths
> Guide me in Your truth
> My hope is in You
> All day long

- What was most meaningful about a past quiet time with God?
- How did you enter this sacred time ... hurriedly, prayerfully, willingly? Explain.
- How was your day prosperous when you unplugged and relinquished control by placing the day in God's competent hands?

Day 14

For this reason, I kneel before the Father, from whom every family in heaven and on earth derives its name. I pray that out of his glorious riches he may strengthen you with power through his Spirit in your inner being, so that Christ may dwell in your hearts through faith— Ephesians 3:14–17.

I depend on God's daily strength to help me complete routine duties, as well as those pre-surgery tasks. To get through decision making, rough days, and the days when I feel less than energetic or beautiful, I ask for His ever-present guidance. In order to sense that inner working Spirit, I consciously decide to walk with God throughout my entire day. My strength comes from being plugged in to the source, God, and not being concerned about what others may think or say. Each of us desperately needs solitude/me-time/play/quiet time.

"Sometimes people need to remind themselves that there is an off-switch—and use it. Solitude is the scarce resource in business lives—having that time when you are disconnected and realizing that everything will go along fine without you," Paul Saffo.

- When do you feel strong and when do you not? What is going on inside you in both cases? Where does your strength come from?
- Do you honestly believe and trust in the one true Father, Creator of you? In what ways can you seek to believe and trust Him?
- Ask God to be your constant companion through the good and bad times. Write out your prayer.

Day 15

The Lord said, Go out and stand on the mountain in the presence of the Lord, for the Lord is about to pass by. Then a great and powerful wind tore the mountains apart and shattered the rocks before the Lord, but the Lord was not in the wind. After the wind there was an earthquake, but the Lord was not in the earthquake. After the earthquake came a fire, but the Lord was not in the fire. And after the fire came a gentle whisper—
1 Kings 19:11, 12.

A compassionate God appeared to Elijah—not in a great and powerful wind, not through an earthquake, nor in the fire, but *after the fire came a gentle whisper* (1 Kings 19:12b). Through that gentle whisper, God spoke to the prophet instructing and encouraging him to continue on with his Father's work. Things were not as terrible as Elijah had imagined. I wonder if such is the case with you and me.

Elijah felt alone, rejected, and tired. He assumed he was the only one left to serve God and *now they are trying to kill me too* (1 Kings 19:10b). Once Elijah finished his pity party, God then gave him his marching orders. Oh, and by the way, there still remained 7,000 in Israel who had not bowed down to Baal. God knows the whole story. Just like Elijah, we don't see the entire picture, but God does!

During Elijah's time, he did not have competing forces such as electronic devices. But other activities and people influenced him away from acknowledging God and His presence. Peace results when I take the time to unplug from this world's constant drone and actively listen to His still, small voice. It is possible that God desires to speak to you in a quiet whisper today.

- Name the last location/time you unplugged from electronic devices, computers and television to filter out this world's distractions? If you cannot remember a time, what plan could you implement to unplug?
- What devices and how many did you unplug from? Was it challenging for you? What obstacles do you anticipate, or did you encounter?
- Journal what you heard, felt, and learned when only silence enveloped you.
- How can you rely on God to take care of the big and little details of your life? List those details you need to turn over to God. Don't delay releasing them to Him.

Prayer of Encouragement:

God, show me those circumstances when I need to step away from modern technology and just **be**. Help me embrace those essential appointments with You regardless of what others might think or say. Regardless of what else is happening around me. A gentle breeze lets me know You are near. You are here listening, watching, and waiting. Thank you. Amen.

I invite you to linger a bit longer over the words in Psalm 46:10. Recording your thoughts, what do they personally mean to you?

Day 11-15   Unplugged From the World

Chapter 4

Don't Worry About Tomorrow

Give your entire attention to what God is doing right now, and don't get worked up about what may or may not happen tomorrow. God will help you deal with whatever hard things come up when the time comes—Matthew 6:34/MSG.

Prioritizing seemed important now that I learned of the tumor behind my eye alongside my brain. Which tasks should be on the top of my list? Scripture teaches ... *do not worry about tomorrow, for tomorrow will worry about itself. Each day has enough trouble of its own* (Matthew 6:34). I know my days are numbered. As I grow older and the body begins to deteriorate, I am beginning to grasp that concept. As a teenager sitting in a church youth group, I remember our pastor asking the stark question.

"So, if this were your last day on planet earth, how would you spend it? Who would you make a point to talk to, visit, or spend time with?"

Wow, such a loaded question for a young person—something I had not thought of or wanted to think about. Besides, I was way too young to die. Death and terminal sickness only happened to old people. At the time, I probably envisioned calling up a few friends and getting together with them for one last hurrah. I doubt spending time with my mom, dad, or siblings came to mind. After all, I saw them all the time and lived with them. They would always be around. Or so I reasoned. However, I received a rude awakening when my mother died of cancer at the early age of fifty-eight. I could not have predicted her early death; otherwise, I'd have done some things differently. A crazy thought plagued me, *Would I live past the age of 58 years? Or, would my life be cut short too, just like my mom?*

Now, many years later, I am faced with the same question. On what and with whom should I be spending my time, energy, and resources? My husband will someday die. Am I spending quality time with him, or do I take him for granted? I realize my Dad grows older and will not live forever. As I plan time with family members and friends, I need to bask in their presence. I realize the importance of being fully present when we get together.

- Are there some things you feel you should be doing differently? Ask God what your priorities should be right now and write them in your journal.
- What does it mean to give your entire attention to God?
- Which tasks can wait until tomorrow?

Prayer of Encouragement:

Lord, show me what my priorities should be at this time. Reveal to me which items on the to-do list need to be done and which can wait. Give me courage to tell others of the hope that lies within me. Grant me confidence and peace to enjoy today and not worry about tomorrow's concerns which may not even happen. Amen.

Day 16

> "Worry does not empty tomorrow of its sorrow; it empties today of its strength," Corrie ten Boom.

How many times have you worried and fretted about a particular concern that never even happened? Or, the results were not nearly as terrible as you'd imagined them to be? Worry robs us of the day's potential joy. Wasted energy. Wasted time. Going straight to God at the beginning of my worry reduces heartache.

The book of Hebrews names those who demonstrated their faith in courageous ways. People such as Noah, Abraham, Sarah, Jacob, Joseph, Moses, and Rahab. By their faith and actions, they chose to do God's will. They didn't always know the reasoning behind their actions. Some saw the immediate result of following God; others did not. Just like us today. We cannot see the entire timeline. Only God knows the beginning and the end.

When I spend my time counting blessings and not airing complaints, benefits seem to multiply. It is wonderful to be free and alive! This is the day the Lord has made; let us rejoice and be glad in it (Psalm 118:24).

I'm so excited. Steve planned a getaway birthday color tour weekend. Since the weather's cooperating, we will be riding our motorcycle up north. I love the fact that the motel rests right on the beach across from the lighthouse in Frankfort. We plan to use the motel as our base camp for two days, ride to Sleeping Bear Dunes and Leland. By not worrying and complaining about what might or might not happen and what I can and cannot do, I am able to enjoy the sights and sounds on my birthday weekend:

Day 16-20   *Don't Worry About Tomorrow*

- Colorful and entertaining Scottsville Clown Band performing in downtown Frankfort parade
- Tour of Point Betsie Lighthouse11 and walking to the very top lookout. Lighthouse crew celebrates the 150-year anniversary of the lighthouse
- Day trip to the picturesque fish town, Leland, where we watched schools of large salmon travel by the docks
- Relaxing picnic lunch by the lighthouse pier of Ludington State Park

Now faith is confidence in what we hope for and assurance about what we do not see. This is what the ancients were commended for—Hebrews 11:1.

- Name the stressors in your life right now.
- Tell Jesus about them asking for His peace that passes all understanding. Compose a prayer for your journal.
- What did you experience as a result of naming your worries?

Day 17

He alone is my rock and my salvation; he is my fortress, I will not be shaken. My salvation and my honor depend on God; he is my mighty rock, my refuge. Trust in him at all times, O people; pour out your hearts to him, for God is our refuge—Psalm 62:6–8.

When I read these words penned by David in the desert of Judah, there is no room for me to worry. *My help and glory are in God—granite-strength and safe-harbor-God—so trust him absolutely* (Psalm 62:6–7/MSG). Granite-strength. Safe harbor. All strong words attributed to a strong God who can shoulder every single care. He cares about me. He cares about my body and how I react during these uncertain times.

Again, I am weary. I desire to be stronger—and not so weary. Worry does that to a body. It causes a body to feel strained and unable to cope. I've heard it said that mental anguish takes its toll and recovery can take longer than a day of physical labor.

Stop and smell the roses, I hear my Lord saying. Pause and gaze out the window. The world passes by. Don't neglect the bird's early morning happy song or the kitty cat purring happily as she naps upon my notes. *You're not too busy to pay attention to details, situations, and people. You have time to digest, eyes to see, and ears to listen to what I have gifted you.*

"Legends say that hummingbirds float free of time, carrying our hopes for love, joy and celebration. The hummingbird's delicate grace reminds us that life is rich, beauty is everywhere, every personal connection has meaning and that laughter is life's sweetest creation," Papyrus.[12]

- What/whom (if anything or anyone) is causing your faith to be shaken?
- What fear are you hesitant to let go of and allow God to handle?
- Take the time to pour your heart out to the One who knows all. Write your words out in the form of a prayer back to Him.

Day 18

And my God will meet all your needs according to the riches of his glory in Christ Jesus— Philippians 4:19.

I decided to attend a writers' conference in the midst of my health issue upheaval. The conference grounds are located on the picturesque shores of Lake Michigan. God affirmed my decision as I walked to the water's edge by the beach. I needed this escape. He spoke to me as I took a break to be alone. A solitary bird perched upon a dock post. Alone. Suddenly, a blue heron majestically soared over the other bird with wings wide open over my head. Alone and solo.

A good share of our life is spent alone. We dress by ourselves, brush our teeth, shower, and eat alone on occasion. The books we choose, we read alone. We study alone, meditate, read Scripture, pray, drive to work and back again alone. If I do not feel good about myself, then life can be miserable. Being concerned about what other human beings feel or think about me can cause depression. Human beings (me included) can be downright nasty and selfish especially when their own needs are being ignored.

God supplied all my needs in the past, maybe not exactly at the time I wanted, but always in His timing. He is never late. I cannot do anything about the past or the future. But I can be present in the present.

> "With the past, I have nothing to do; nor with the future. I live now,"
> Ralph Waldo Emerson.

- When was the last time you complained to God? What was your complaint(s)?
- What need do you continue to obsess about?
- What blessings can you name? Thank God with a prayer of praise in your journal.

Day 19

Are not five sparrows sold for two pennies? Yet not one of them is forgotten by God. Indeed, the very hairs of your head are all numbered. Don't be afraid; you are worth more than many sparrows—Luke 12:6.

My first thought when I opened my eyes: just roll over and try to go back to sleep. Instead, I grabbed my journal and Bible. I wanted God's voice to reign in my head and heart. I wanted the first voice I heard this morning to be His. Instead of counting sheep, I chose to count my blessings and name them one by one in my bedside journal.

Confusion and conflict crowd their way into my brain. Yes, even in the midst of semi-isolation. As I think through the day ahead, I am more concerned over how I look and whether my outfit matches or not. The others in my life really do not care or notice what style I'm wearing or not wearing. *Why do I obsess over such trivial matters?*

Since God cares for me so much, I don't have to spend needless waking moments fretting about items I have no control over. Those thoughts cause frustration and annoyance. I give all my thoughts over to God; just let go and let God.

- How long do you spend in front of the mirror on a daily basis stewing over the externals? Consider if the time spent fretting over externals is really necessary.
- How dependent on God are you for adequate clothing and food? Explain.
- What worry pops into your head that you need to pray about?

Day 20

Do not worry about your life, what you will eat; or about your body, what you will wear. For life is more than food, and the body more than clothes. Consider the ravens: They do not sow or reap, they have no storeroom or barn; yet God feeds them. And how much more valuable you are than birds! Who of you by worrying can add a single hour to your life? Since you cannot do this very little thing, why do you worry about the rest? —Luke 12:22–26.

On day two of the writers' conference, I became feverish and sick which landed me in bed wrapped in blankets. My caring roommate, Noreen, attended to me bringing what food and drink I could handle. She even offered to drive me home if I wanted to go. I chose to remain at the conference in hopes the bug would pass quickly. Deferring her own needs and health, she compassionately cared for me. Thankfully, I recovered and was able to enjoy the remainder of the conference.

When I regained strength, I marched on into the conference with my head held high expecting God to disclose His vision and great truths. My desire is to carry on with His mission of writing through me. Regardless of anything and everything going on in my life, I just needed to be at the conference. I needed to let it all go and be present here and now. James Watkins[13] suggests using

God as your Holy-Ghost writer. "God's primary desire is not that we write about Him, or even for Him, it's that we write with Him."[14]

"If you worry about what might be, and wonder what might have been, you will ignore what is," Unknown.

- In your spare time, what do you immediately turn to first … the computer; absent-mindedly flip the television remote, your Bible, devotional, etc.?
- When did you last spend time engaged in a productive, positive activity? What did you do?
- How much time do you concentrate on doing what pleases God? Do you desire to spend more or less time doing this? Why?

Prayer of Encouragement:

Dear God, thank you for putting guardian angels in my life to care for me. I know You are in control of my life. Help me put aside health issues and concentrate on what You have prepared for me. I willingly accept the path You've charted in my life. Whatever the outcome, I choose to praise You. Amen.

Read about encouragements and warnings in Luke, Chapter 12.

Day 16-20   Don't Worry About Tomorrow

Chapter 5

How Big is My God?

I had exactly one week to go before brain surgery. My mind spiraled in twenty different directions. *Would I see my daughter marry? Would I experience the birth of a grandchild?* These questions and more bombarded my mind. No one could say for sure that I wouldn't experience complications, seizures, or develop further problems after removal of the tumor.

A registration nurse from the hospital called to ask several questions. She asked about current symptoms I may be experiencing, who would care for me afterward, and gave information regarding day before and day of surgery instructions.

"You seem pretty calm about the surgery. Are you afraid?" the nurse said.

I took a deep breath and said, "Oh yes, I'm afraid. It does help when I put it all in the hands of God, the Great Physician."

Just how big is my God? He is big enough to carry me through surgery and recovery. Since God's shoulders are big enough to carry any burden, I can unload on Him. I need only ask Him, and that incomparable peace permeates my heart and mind. God is ready and willing to replace my fears with His peace. He never promised there would be no pain, but He said He would walk through the valley with me (Psalm 23).

He has never let me down in the past. Early in our marriage, God protected me by sparing my life during a serious car accident. He provided comfort and hope at the death of my mother. I felt His strength while prayerfully loving a wayward teenager. Why should I doubt Him now? God answered prayers during those tumultuous times and soothed my soul. My responsibility is to give my fears to God.

Just before leaving my position at work, the organization chose a new boss. He supported my decision to leave and showed empathy and understanding in a non-judgmental way. Rich shared with me that he had undergone three brain surgeries. Only God could have paired us! He wrote out a few special Bible verses that helped him and suggested I insert my name making the words personal.

Teresa, *do not be anxious about anything, but in everything, by prayer and petition, with thanksgiving, present your requests to God. And the peace of God, which transcends all understanding, will guard your hearts and your minds in Christ Jesus ... I* [Teresa] *can do all things through Christ who strengthens me*—Philippians 4:6–7, 13.

I've been reading Charles Stanley's New York Times bestseller, *Finding Peace—God's Promise of a Life Free From Regret, Anxiety, and Fear.* Words of encouragement soothe my mind and soul in the midst of an uncertain outcome. For me, it is easier to focus on connecting with God first thing in the morning or before bedtime. In the morning, my mind is a blank slate ready to accept my mission for the day. In the evening, Scripture allows me to unwind from a day of stimulation and calm my racing thoughts.

Stanley includes a quote from Oswald Chambers: "When it begins to dawn on my conscious life what God's purpose is, there is the laughter of the possibility of the impossible. The impossible is exactly what God does." With God the impossible is possible—there is nothing too big for God to handle. Stanley also says, "Our God is a great and limitless God. He dwells in eternity and operates in infinity. He has all things within His understanding and all things under His control."

- How is God helping you during a rough patch? Be specific.
- Who or what in your life causes great anxiety and stress?
- Can you recall a time God helped you in the past? For me, it helps to recall those past rescues and gives me hope and persistence to keep on praying, waiting, and believing.
- What steps can you take to guard your heart and mind?

Prayer of Encouragement:

Father, help me see beyond my current circumstances to the big picture. Give me wisdom and faith to believe, even though I am weak. I remember the times You came through for me in the past. Times when I did not think I would make it beyond an hour or a day. Regardless of the outcome, You have ALL things under Your control. I chose to trust and obey. Amen.

Day 21

For with God nothing shall be impossible—Luke 1:37/KJV.

This evening my hubby and I watch a beautiful sunset over the pier and lighthouse. Steve photographed and I read in between gazing at the magnificent horizon. The night proved clear as we watched tiny bright lights in the sky come into focus one by one. I never want to forget the colors of fall: red, yellow, orange, or the remaining green, grassy fields. Dry, brown and yellow corn stalks and sunflower fields. So much to absorb, compliment, and appreciate. We walked together and alone, rested some, ate food, and enjoyed God's fall creation handiwork.

Consider the words to the famous song written by Chris Tomlin, *How Great is Our God*. Only five one-syllable words, but the words are packed with power and meaning. Let's look at a few attributes of this great and awesome God:

- Clothed in majesty (compared to my filthy rags)
- He is Light (I sometimes hide in darkness, how about you?)
- King of all Kings (I am nothing without Him)

When I humble myself and call on His matchless name, I am called a daughter of the most high King. God desires my fellowship and bids me to walk in the light as He is in the light. He truly is a great God—worthy of all my praise.

- When you think about God, what character traits come to mind?
- Do you realize none of your worries are too big or too small for Him to handle? Name the most recent concern you shared with God.
- Do you sincerely believe with all your heart and soul that God is big enough to handle this problem? If so, what proof would others see that you believe?

Day 22

An angel of the Lord appeared to them, and the glory of the Lord shone around them, and they were terrified. But the angel said to them, Do not be afraid. I bring you good news of great joy that will be for all the people—Luke 2:9–10.

Doubts and fears about the upcoming surgery continue to pop into my head. *Will my family sense peace in me as I go forward? Or witness panic? I wonder if the outcome will be positive.* The surgeons can speculate about a favorable prognosis, but until after the surgery, no one knows for sure, except for God. He is in the business of healing and comfort. Even when my finite mind cannot see His hand at work, I need not worry because He has my best interest in mind.

God is with me, watching, guiding, enabling and equipping me to do my very best. He's still working on me. I recall the angel's comforting words announcing Christ's birth to the shepherds. If I make verse 10 in Luke 2 personal, it would read: *Do not be afraid*, Teresa. Feel free to fill in your name here. Make it personal and directed right to you.

- Is there a fear you are holding on to? (Maybe, you've clasped the fear tightly for months or even years). Name that fear.
- Can you release your grasp on the fears long enough to offer them up to God who is in charge of the big and the little stuff? Will you dare release the fear right now?
- Write a prayer to God letting go of a fear.

Day 23

Ah, Sovereign Lord, you have made the heavens and the earth by your great power and outstretched arm. Nothing is too hard for you. Then the word of the LORD came to Jeremiah: I am the LORD, the God of all mankind. Is anything too hard for me?—Jeremiah 32:17, 26-27.

On my morning walk, I notice color in the sky hovering over the lake. Pale, pinkish tones ever so gently signal a new sunrise. It's as if God is saying: *Good morning, sleepyhead. Rise and shine and give Me the glory. I have great things in store for you, but you must do the work. Trust Me.*

All my striving, pushing, and planning are no match for my Heavenly Father. I can do nothing aside from His permission. God made me who I am today. There is nothing God cannot do—even things which do not make sense to humans. He did not need to call a meeting or hire a team of experts to analyze the situation. God spoke and the entire universe appeared. And that universe includes you and me.

- What/who makes you feel impatient? In what way? Formulate your list in your journal.

- Do you believe God created the fish in the sea, the birds of the air, and that He cares for you even more than all of those combined? How do you know God cares for you? Consider these words, *Look at the birds of the air; they do not sow or reap or store away in barns, and yet your heavenly Father feeds them. Are you not much more valuable than they? Can any one of you by worrying add a single hour to your life?* (Matthew 6:26, 27).

- In what area of your life do you need to trust Him more?

Day 24

God has said, never will I leave you; never will I forsake you. So we say with confidence, The Lord is my helper; I will not be afraid. What can mere mortals do to me?—Hebrews 13:5-6.

My cell phone vibrated during a meeting. At the next break, I called the number back. A staff person from the medical records office called to set me up for surgery. After asking routine questions, she then added,

"You have a great attitude about this. You're really brave!"

"No, not really—just trusting my God who brought me this far. My doctor found the tumor, now we have to get it out of there. I don't feel brave. But I am confident God is present and knows about the whole situation." Through this process, I'm finding a bit more bravery each new day. An inner prompting goes something like this, *Now is the time. There's no time like the present to give Me the glory than during these circumstances.* And He's right.

Day 21-25   *How Big is My God?*

No matter what you face today, cling to the promise God will never fail or abandon you. Cry out to God. He listens, hears, and responds. God cares for you above all others and waits for you. He can and will help. You need not be afraid. You may think back to a parent or trusted friend who was not always there for you, or worse, abused you or someone you love. Maybe they abandoned you or they were in the picture, but really did not pay attention to you the way they should have. Be careful not to compare their inability to love properly to the Heavenly Father's love. There is no comparison. No one compares to God and what He offers you.

God will provide a way of escape. Sometimes He will remove us from the storm (whatever yours may be: abuse, abandonment, health issues). Or, circumstances may not change, but God rides out the storm with His beloved. God always gave me an out. Sometimes I did not acknowledge or follow through with the escape route. Those are times I ended up sorry I did not choose the right path. When I chose God's way out, relief flooded my mind, body, and soul. Release your worries and give them back to Him. Whatever you may be dealing with today, this too is your perfect escape.

Maybe you are in the middle of a crossroads. Ask yourself, "Do I continue in this path of doing my own thing my way regardless of who I hurt? Or, do I follow God's leading and trust Him knowing He wants only the best?" He's not a joy-killer; but a joy-filler.

For God hath not given us the spirit of fear; but of power, and of love, and of a sound mind— 2 Timothy 1:7/KJV.

- What steps can you take to allow God to be your helper?
- Cry out in confidence to God and tell Him about your sorrow and doubt. Write in your journal.
- Describe a time when you felt God's spirit of power, love, and sound mind.

Day 25

But do not forget this one thing, dear friends: With the Lord a day is like a thousand years, and a thousand years are like a day. The Lord is not slow in keeping his promise, as some understand slowness. Instead, he is patient with you, not wanting anyone to perish, but everyone to come to repentance—2 Peter 3:8–9.

I catch myself wondering out loud, *Why doesn't this or that happen right now? I need this to happen now. I want it now. My body isn't working as it should—do You know, or do You care, God?* I often forget God does not operate on the same timetable as I do.

Maybe you wait for a special person to ask for your hand in marriage. Does your heart ache for a wayward spouse or child who chose a different path than you'd hoped for? Do not despair. We cannot permit this waiting to rob us of today's joy. Every day that God awakens you is cause for rejoicing with a thankful heart. He cares when the tears and deep hurts occur. One day to Him is like many, many years. Rest assured, He's got it all figured out and knows the beginning from the end.

In the second book of Peter, God calls me a dear friend. Beloved. Such terms of endearment I do not deserve because of my sin. Yet He remains long-suffering. Knowing this brings refreshment and renewal to my soul. If God is

Day 21-25   How Big is My God?

on my side, then I can go on. God shows up exactly when He needs to show up. Not a minute too early or too late.

"Even the strongest and bravest must sometimes weep. It shows they have a great heart, one that can feel compassion for others," Brian Jacques.[15]

- Are you waiting for some big event to take place to the exclusion of enjoying today? Name that event.
- What does your heart ache for: a wayward spouse, a child, financial peace, depression or some other burden? Name your specific heartache.
- What specific burden will you transfer over to a God? Write a prayer of transfer.

Prayer of Encouragement:
    Dear God, I know Your timetable is not mine, but sometimes I forget. I am short-sighted and narrow-minded. Forgive me. Whether you choose for me to live another day or 10 or 20 years—You know best. I truly long to let go and let You handle life's circumstances. When I am weak, You are strong! Thank you.

Think about your relationship with God and that He calls you a *dear friend* in 2 Peter 3:8.

Chapter 6

Think on These Things

He brought me out into a spacious place; he rescued me because he delighted in me—
Psalm 18:19.

God delights in me? No way—me, a mere flawed human being? The fact that the great, awesome and powerful God would stoop so low as to free me, rescue me, and then delight in me is almost incomprehensible. When I begin to count the number of times I've disappointed God, well, the number is too great to tally. And I continue to disappoint.

Think about the word delight. The definition of delight is a high degree of pleasure; joy, to have or take great pleasure. Synonyms of the word delight are to please, gratify, rejoice, gladden, tickle, satisfy, content, charm, allure, and attract. Even when I do not act kind or loving, He still loves me. When I jump to conclusions about a family member or my neighbor's actions not knowing her motive or heart, God still loves me.

Have you been through deep waters? While anticipating my upcoming surgery, friends offer recommendations such as hospital treatment facilities that worked for them or their friends. They tell me they are praying. My son tells me he is praying and fasting along with others in Minnesota. I've received numerous phone calls, e-mails, and notes from within the state and beyond. These tokens of love mean so much to me. Aunt Jackie said she's there for me in spirit and affirmed she knows God is present too. She went a bit further to say,

"Never forget that you are a Writer. Your new assignment may be to log your journey for others to see and learn." And you know, I believe she's right.

I cannot depend on my physical body to perform properly at all times. I grow weary and weak, and depend on others to get me through the day. Memorizing Scripture (which it not easy for me) carries me through ordinary and not-so-ordinary life occurrences.

David, the writer of Psalm 18, knew what it meant to be lonely and in need of rescue. As an outlaw, David fled for his life on more than one occasion. Acts 13:22 speaks of David *the son of Jesse, a man after My own heart, who will do all My will*. Still, the anointed king over Judah and Israel was not perfect. David sinned and made moral mistakes struggling to do what he knew to be right. After confession of sin, King David enjoyed spiritual and physical restoration with his God. God does not abandon His people. *Everyone who calls on the name of the Lord will be saved* (Acts 2:21).

You may be walking through a dark valley or in the middle of a storm. Sometimes God takes us out of the valley; other times He walks through the valley with us. Either way, He does not leave us stranded. Apart from this great God, I can do nothing; with Him all things are possible. *If my people who are called by my name will humble themselves and pray and seek my face and turn from their wicked ways, I will hear from heaven and will forgive their sins and restore their land.*[16]

"We have to trust that our stories deserve to be told. We may discover that the better we tell our stories the better we will want to live them," Henri Nouwen

- What Scripture can you recite and claim affirming you are His and He is yours? Write those references in your journal. If a verse does not come to mind, here are a few to consider: Hebrews 13:5, Nehemiah 1:9, Psalm 46:1-3, and Psalm 56:3-4.
- Name an example when you knew God rescued you? Stop. Take a few minutes to thank Him for divine intervention in your life.
- Write out your prayer of thanksgiving.

Prayer of Encouragement:

Thank you, God, for rescuing me. For those times, I knew You rescued me and other times I had no clue. Your great love and mercy chose to free me in spite of myself. My heart's desire is to run to You sooner next time. I'm thankful You take great delight in me as a uniquely created human being. When the deep waters threaten to swallow me up, I long for You to be my strong support so You may delight in me all the days of my life. Amen.

Day 26

Finally, brothers and sisters, whatever is true, whatever is noble, whatever is right, whatever is pure, whatever is lovely, whatever is admirable—if anything is excellent or praiseworthy—think about such things. Whatever you have learned or received or heard from me, or seen in me—put it into practice. And the God of peace will be with you—Philippians 4:8–9.

The Apostle Paul reminds us in Philippians to fix our mind and eyes on wholesome qualities such as truth, honor, purity, and things of praise. Rejoice with Paul and rededicate yourself to finding joy in Christ. What I fix my mind and eyes on ultimately becomes what I think and eventually end up acting upon.

Day 26-30   *Think on These Things*

What things are true in your life? Relax in the knowledge that God is a personal God. He cares enough about me (and you) to reach *down from on high and took hold of me; he drew me out of deep waters. He rescued me from my powerful enemy, from my foes, who were too strong for me. They confronted me in the day of my disaster, but the Lord was my support* (Psalm 18:16–18).

"We become what we think about all day long,"
Ralph Waldo Emerson.

- How can you keep focused on God? List ideas that come to mind. What would be the benefits?
- Is there something/someone in your life you are clinging to that is not right or wholesome for you? Name this thing/person that you refuse to relinquish. Consider this may be the time and place to let go of what/whom you cling to so desperately.
- Ponder a few praiseworthy and pure things in your life that come to mind. Create a list to review from time to time. Practice thanking God for these entries —Scripture says the God of peace will be with you.
-

Day 27

Whatever is right ... think about such things—Philippians 4:8.

The definition of righteous is: honorable, blameless, moral, good, just, respectable. Does my life characterize these virtues? Not always. I often fall short of God's expectations. During those times, I need to confess the sin to Him. Sometimes I do good deeds so others may see how much time or money I contributed. God does not approve of doing right for the wrong reasons.

My co-worker tells me I weigh heavy on her heart. She assures me she brings my name before God's throne as she prays for me. Laur says God has not brought me this far to let me go, and that He will walk through this ordeal with me. "The Lord gives trying situations to those who are strong and mature in the faith enough to handle trials. But, He also gives us family and friends to support and pray with us too." She goes on to tell me that my ministry is different now. Others are watching to see how I act or react. Will anyone detect that I am a Christian by my love and actions?

"Whether you think you can or can't, you're right," Henry Ford.

- Can you think of something you should be doing (or not doing) that you know is the right thing, but have been ignoring the Holy Spirit's prompting? Journal those thoughts.
- Name two actions taken recently that would cause an observer to believe you are a Christian.
- What can you do to become stronger and more mature in your faith?

Day 26-30   Think on These Things

Day 28

Whatever is pure ... think about such things. Whatever you have learned or received or heard from me, or seen in me—put it into practice. And the God of peace will be with you— Philippians 4:8-9.

> "Watch your thoughts for they become words.
> Watch your words for they become actions.
> Watch your actions for they become habits.
> Watch your habits for they become your character.
> And watch your character for it becomes your destiny,"
> Margaret Thatcher.

What do you think of when you hear the word pure or purity? Pure water, silver, or a purebred animal? How about chastity in marriage or in dating? According to Webster, to be pure is to be clean, untainted, wholesome, and chaste. How often do you hear the word chaste in today's world? Spotless, faithful, virtuous ... rarely used words.

When my son and daughter-in-law met and started courting, they decided to save their first kiss until the wedding day. I wondered at the logistics of that commitment fearing failure and the consequence of guilty feelings. But by the grace of God; Andrew and Bethany kept that original promise! What a sweet union and reminder as we witnessed their wedding day. They saved themselves for each other.

The beauty of a purity commitment is that you can start right now. Regardless of past history, today is a brand-new day to make that purity promise. Our God is a God of second chances. He looks favorably upon a sincere heart committed to change. To live for Him in unrushed awe as we serve. Be blessed this day.

Two things to remember:
1. Take care of your thoughts when you are alone
2. Take care of your words when you are with people[17]

- What area of your life needs cleaning up?
- How might you experience peace and contentment by choosing a vow of purity and faithfulness?
- What things can you think on that would create a visual of pureness and nobility?

Day 29

Whatever is lovely ... meditate on these things—Philippians 4:8/NKJV.

When I consider something that is lovely, my mind returns to a vacation several years ago. While relaxing, I witnessed a radiant sunrise and multicolored sunset over the Gulf of Mexico shoreline. The sun appeared to disappear beneath the ocean. The God of Creation shared His magnificent handiwork with anyone who took time to observe. I stood amazed and thankful.

Back in Michigan after many long months of dark, cold days and nights, we long for the first sight of spring. The crocus is the first flower to pop its hardy head due to being sheltered close to my home's foundation. At the first sign of spring, my heart leaps because I know warmer sun-filled days lurk just around the corner.

I would encourage you to look into a song written by Matt Redman entitled, *Your Grace Finds Me*. The song speaks of God's great grace. Grace that finds me and you on the mountaintop, in the everyday and the mundane. *It's there in the newborn cry ... there in the light of every sunrise.* Look for God's grace in the sorrow and the dancing. His grace is all around if we take the time to seek it, its *there on a wedding day, ... in the weeping by the graveside.*

> "Sometimes we need to go where we can hear a screen door slam, echoes of our parents calling our name, wish on a falling star and catch fireflies in a jar," Connie Sue.

- What (if anything) are you fixing your mind on that is unlovely or unpleasant?
- Are you ready and willing to let go of offensive and unhealthy thoughts? If so, then do it with God's strength and grace. Write your prayer of release.
- What images can you fix your thoughts on as a reminder that our God prefers lovely, authentic, and praiseworthy meditation?

Day 30

If anything is excellent or praiseworthy—think about such things ... And the God of peace will be with you—Philippians 4:8-9.

Sports players who achieve the most goals or points are held in high esteem. Talk of beauty and fame bombard the Internet and news waves. Hollywood celebrities receive nominations for acting, producing and praise for just showing up. Much chatter takes place about who is wearing which designer's creation. Conversations abound regarding how fabulous they look (or don't look) in which color and style.

When I consider what is excellent or deserving of praise, I think of someone who faithfully, and without complaint, cares for an elderly family member. Or, a dedicated parent who thanklessly, without complaint, cares year after year for a special child's needs. Feeding and providing safe shelter for orphans, widows, the homeless and abused would rank high on God's chart of excellent deeds. Those who do these selfless deeds should be admired and truly worthy of praise. The God of peace promises to reside with us when we think on and do what we know to be good and right. I cannot think of a higher calling or promise than this.

God sees the little things that others may not see or understand. Consider the widow's two mites (or very small copper coins) story described in Luke 21:1–4. Others put their money in to be noticed; she put in the little she had. They gave a tiny part of their abundant surplus; she contributed out of her lack. Scripture states *this poor widow has put in more than all the others. All these people gave their gifts out of their wealth; but she out of her poverty put in all she had to live on.* The widow's heart did not go unnoticed. Deep down, she gave her all. Can this be said of you or me? Do I give in a generous and sacrificial manner? Willingly,

Day 26-30 *Think on These Things*

without compulsion? Do we give of our money, time, and talents beyond convenience or safety?[18]

> "Our prayers may be awkward. Our attempts may be feeble. But since the power of prayer is in the One who hears it and not in the one who says it, our prayers make a difference," Max Lucado.

- Remember a time when you gave of yourself in either time or money to serve the less fortunate. Write about the experience.
- Is there someone in your sphere of influence who could use a helping hand or a kind word? What can you do for them?
- Pray and ask God for an opportunity to reach out to someone in need. Write your prayer in your journal.

Prayer of Encouragement:

Dear God, flood my mind with noble, good, and honest thoughts without consideration of public acclamation or accolades. Purge my mind and heart of corrupt and negative thoughts. I cannot do this alone. I desperately need You to accomplish this purging task of mind contamination. Thank you in advance for Your mighty works. Amen.

Happiness depends on happenings, but joy depends on Christ. As you read chapter 4 of Philippians (Paul's joy letter), look for three topics: rejoicing, prayer, and contentment.

NOTES

Section 2

Body (Life is Fragile)

Chapter 7

Escape and Enjoy Life!

Praise the Lord, O my soul. O Lord my God, you are very great; you are clothed with splendor and majesty. He wraps himself in light as with a garment; he stretches out the heavens like a tent and lays the beams of his upper chambers on their waters, He makes the clouds his chariot and rides on the wings of the wind—Psalm 104:1–3.

Looking past the shores of the Pacific Ocean, it's easy to see God's greatness. Who could create such beauty? Just like the hairs on my head are numbered, each grain of sand is recorded and every creature counted. There is a distinct division between where the water ends and the sky begins. Dry land separates from the rolling waves, just as He promised in the book of Genesis.

The reality and relaxation of vacation sets in after a few days. It takes sheer willpower combined with a deliberate choice to put all electronics aside. Willing these moments to be without the distraction of modern technology.

Peaches and cream colored sand beneath my toes, diversely shaped shells, and teal-blue Caribbean waves entice me to forget my homeland. My eyes marvel at living creatures that are unfamiliar to me such as iguanas, peacocks and wild monkeys. Even the foliage—cacti, vibrant pink and purple flowers—beg me to learn their names. The chatter of various bird and animal sounds in the jungle causes me to pause and listen intently. Human voices around me speak in varied tongues, which I do not comprehend.

The southern sun and breeze warm me. Mind, body, and soul relax as stress and responsibility trickle down like sweat beads. Taking in the vastness of the water, ocean and waves—boundless and limitless just like God's love. Lap after lap, no end to the tide coming in and going out. One continuous motion with no beginning or end—just like my God! My mind cannot comprehend such power and majesty. God spoke and it was so without an architect meeting or conference discussions.

Feelings of great joy permeate my soul as I gaze upon such magnificence. I can place my trust and whole being in a God who created an entire universe for humankind to enjoy. He spoke creation into existence in only six days. My response can be nothing short of awe and appreciation.

- Remembering a past excursion, in what ways did you feel your worries evaporate? Record your thoughts in your journal/notebook.
- Where might you go to witness God's creation?
- Plan a trip to an escape location, near or far, where you can relax. Sit and meditate on the wonders surrounding you.

Prayer of Encouragement:

Thank you, God, for this opportunity to witness Your majesty in the beauty around me. May I not forget your goodness and love. I choose to focus on Your beauty and not on uncertain circumstances.

Day 31

By yourself you're unprotected. With a friend you can face the worst. Can you round up a third? A three-stranded rope isn't easily snapped—Ecclesiastes 4:12/MSG.

As I think back to when my children were young, I miss those evening chats, bedtime stories, and prayers. Children innocently verbalize their heart's dreams whether big or small. They rarely hold back their fears and feelings. Now that my daughter's grown up, we try to plan a yearly overnight outing.

Adult children are more like equals. Just two adults enjoying time away together. They learn there is another mom inside this mom—a fun-loving, compassionate individual bursting to come out to be seen and heard. I love pre-planning the possibilities of our destination site. We often walk the pier to a lighthouse, peruse crafty or second hand stores and flea markets. Amanda and I competitively take pictures of lovely flowers or scenery, and enjoy delectable meals. One getaway, we treated ourselves to a relaxing massage. On those outings, the two of us can talk unhindered by everyday distractions.

My daughter wisely points out, "An excursion needn't be far from your home front. It may just be a walk in your neighborhood, or stepping out into the garden to enjoy the sights, sounds, and smells. What about packing a lunch for one and drive to the beach or water's edge? The point is to find an escape location that will put your mind and body at ease. Take the time to re-charge and reset."

There's something about an overnight trip that feels like a real adventure ready to make new memories. Maybe it's the physical activity of packing an overnight bag, or the total change of scenery leaving the known and comfortable setting. Like a sailor when he unties the bowlines and allows the wind to take the boat to unexplored places. This liberty sets mind and soul free from ordinary routines of life.

> "If you want to go fast, go alone. If you want to go far, go together," African Proverb.

- When you read the African proverb above, what thoughts or emotions run through your mind? Are you someone who desires to go fast all the time, or would you rather go far together in community?
- Who might you ask to escape with if even for a few hours? In what way do you feel safe and secure in the location you find yourself?
- Plan to spend part of this occasion soaking up fresh air and journaling your observations using all your senses: sight, sound, smell, touch, and taste.

Day 32

Though one may be overpowered, two can defend themselves. A cord of three strands is not quickly broken—Ecclesiastes 4:12.

A few years ago, my brother and sister planned our first sibling reunion. We planned to meet in Baton Rouge, Louisiana, where our Uncle Carrol and Aunt Dorothy lived. My brother, Lonnie, flew from California and my sister, Karen, and I flew from Michigan. In addition, we took a day trip to New Orleans sampling beignets and jambalaya as we listened to street musicians and watched artists create.

We reminded each other we were not getting any younger. My sister had recently fractured her right shoulder, so she could have easily passed on the opportunity to join us. But no, we persevered together. Since she had very little mobility in her arm, I buckled her seat belt in the plane and pushed her bag along in the airport.

Our uncle and aunt treated us to famous Louisiana seafood cuisine including alligator appetizer, crawfish, and Cajun hush puppies. Family welcomed us with open arms. We lingered long as we said our third and fourth good-byes; just one more hug and we are on our way. No pretense or prior expectations, just pure joy, love, and immediate sanctuary—a trip to remember for life. We promised to strive to make it happen again.

Trust in the Lord, and do good; so you will dwell in the land, and enjoy security. Take delight in the Lord, and he will give you the desires of your heart—Psalm 37:3–4/RSV.

- Who will you ask to stand with you in times of trouble? Why do you choose that particular person(s)?
- Jot down ideas on how you plan to take delight in God today?
- What desire(s) burns in your heart?

Day 31-35   *Escape and Enjoy Life!*

Day 33

A person standing alone can be attacked and defeated, but two can stand back-to-back and conquer. Three are even better, for a triple-braided cord is not easily broken—
Ecclesiastes 4:12/NLT.

    I have a couple of good friends who invite me to escape with them from time to time. One friend invited me to her cabin up north near Sleeping Bear Dunes.[19] Deep, pure white snow covered the ground, but that did not prevent us from taking a brisk walk to explore God's winter handiwork. We felt at ease and comfortable eating simple meals and snacks. Lounging in front of a toasty-warm stone fireplace, we munched on popcorn, relived tales from the past, and shared future dreams. Regardless of how long the separation, it seems like only yesterday when we come together again.

    As crazy as it sounds; we found joy while visiting the local hardware store. In the middle of a small nearly deserted lakeshore town, this shop exhibited Christmas in full array: snow frosted trees and evergreen plants tied with festive ribbons. Christmas treasures awaited our discovery. Our addictive laughter spread as we proudly wore our just purchased up-north matching goofy hats. A clerk took our picture in front of the resident life-size stuffed moose. What fun and in a *hardware store*. With heart's door open to joy and adventure, those positive emotions came alive. After a contented slumber, I journaled:

Life is: Good Fragile Precious

Home Away from Home

Comfortable, safe
All the niceties of home
No detail overlooked
Kick back
Shoes off

Crackling fire in fireplace
Bowl full of buttery popcorn
Words flow effortlessly
Talk of past, present and
Dreams for future

Causes me to remember a place
Called home so long ago

Now we make the memories
For our children and grandchildren

No expectations
No worry
No judgment felt
Free to be me
Exactly what God intended
Most importantly,
Just to **be**

Day 31-35   Escape and Enjoy Life!

- Do you remember the last time you experienced this type of blessed peace described in the above story? Describe the peace and how it affected your mind, body, and soul.
- Would a certain attitude or action be helpful to position yourself properly to accept God's peace?
- Ask God to create time for a retreat (near or far). List blessings received from escaping and enjoying life.

Day 34

You will keep him in perfect peace, whose mind is stayed on You, because he trusts in You— Isaiah 26:3/NKJV.

A few sources of pleasure and pain …

Pleasure:	embarking on a mother-daughter overnight adventure
Pain:	when someone fails to rejoice with me
Pleasure:	feeling the sun kiss my cheek
Pain:	feeling cold, wet rain descend from a dark, cloudy sky
Pleasure:	a smile or giggle from a baby or child
Pain:	a child's tears
Pleasure:	catching an hour cat-nap in the middle of the day
Pain:	inability to turn my brain off when I should be sleeping
Pleasure:	being available, flexible, and willing to follow God's direction
Pain:	when words cannot convey what is on my heart (though sometimes that's okay; see illustration in next section)

Then they sat on the ground with him for seven days and nights. No one said a word to Job, for they saw that his suffering was too great for words—Job 2:13/NLT.

I see several tips in this passage to help encourage someone going through stormy times.

1. **Observance.** A friend saw Job's suffering. Open eyes/open heart. Availability in bodily form, not just throwing out a few flippant words, "Let me know if I can help you." Be specific. For example,
    a. I can watch your children next Tuesday or Wednesday. Or, I could do your laundry.
    b. What day can I bring a meal over to you? Are there any allergies I need to take into consideration?

2. **Time.** Job's friends sat with him. Coming alongside and just sitting turned out to be the best and most helpful. In fact, at the end of the book of Job, God commends those men who did just this.

3. **Endurance.** Seven days and seven nights. That's a long time to sit on the ground and say nothing. They did not say a quick, perfunctory, "so sorry for your loss." Those friends were in this for the long haul.

Silence. No one said a word. Sometimes the best thing to say is nothing even though our first inclination is to fix the situation in an attempt to take away the pain. There weren't enough words or the right words to convey to Job how deep of a loss he must have felt. Job lost nearly everything: his oxen and donkeys attacked by Sabeans from southwest Arabia, sheep and servants killed by fire, and more servants lost by the sword. His sons and daughters died when a mighty wind collapsed the house they were feasting in. To compound matters, Job became inflicted *with painful sores from the soles of his feet to the top of his head* (Job 2:7). Even his wife became exasperated with him. Yet, through all of this, *Job did not sin in what he said* (Job 2:10). Can you imagine such a person as Job? What a shining example of accepting the good and bad.

When we take the initiative and time to come alongside someone hurting, both our burdens are lightened. Blessings flow two ways during this win-win situation. Your friend enjoys a brief escape while you help shoulder his load. Most of the time our friends do not want a solution. Just demonstrate you care by showing up and lend a listening ear. The Holy Spirit will guide you to the next step as you surrender your agenda and allow His leading.

- Who in your life could benefit from a few hours of your time, use a helping hand, or a listening ear? Make your list and go to God asking Him to enlarge your territory—to enlarge your life so you can make a greater impact[20] (more influence, more responsibility, and more opportunity to make a mark for God.)
- Describe the last time you felt at perfect peace in the midst of pain. Record those sacred thoughts.
- Take time to pray and share with God the intimate needs of your heart. One such prayer appears in the book of 1 Chronicles 4:10. Jabez cried out to the God of Israel, *Oh, that you would bless me and enlarge my territory! Let your hand be with me, and keep me from harm so that I will be free from pain. And God granted his request.*

Day 35

A man of many companions may come to ruin, but there is a friend who sticks closer than a brother—Proverbs 18:24.

"I'll be camping at the lake. Would you like to join me for some girl time?" asks my friend.

"Would I? Oh my, that sounds glorious. Are you sure? I don't want to interrupt your precious me-time either."

"Now girlfriend, you know me by now. I wouldn't ask you if I didn't sincerely want you to come. You need something else to think about besides your upcoming surgery."

What else did I have going on? Could it wait? YES, it would have to wait! I'd been neglecting girlfriend and me-time. All sorts of thoughts bombarded my brain. This would be a priority for the next two days. Did I have second thoughts? Of course. Did I regret going? Absolutely not!

I knew I'd made the right decision the moment I entered the campground. My friend eagerly awaited my arrival. As soon as I pulled up, I saw her relaxing in a comfortable chair with a book in her lap. *Ahhhhh, that's the life*, I thought. When she saw me drive up, she immediately came over and gave me a big hug.

"I'm so glad you came."

"So am I. **So am I!**"

We talked and talked. No expectations, no worries entered my head. Deep breaths helped me merge into relaxation mode. After catching up, we walked a well-worn path to Lake Michigan causing me to put thoughts of my brain tumor on hold. If I chose to bring the subject up, she was happy to talk about my fears. That's what friends do. They sense your mood and spirit without speaking a word. Sometimes no words or silence equal just the precise remedy.

Day 31-35   *Escape and Enjoy Life!*

The two of us enjoyed a simple lunch. We relaxed under the welcoming shade of pine trees in lounge chairs reading, writing, or simply snoozing. The sun cast rainbow colors over the water and land as we strolled along the beach and marveled at God's handiwork.

Sleep comes easily as the sun sets and my body begins to charge down. I slept better and longer than at home in my own bed. With a friend, I can face the world. I have someone to bounce ideas off and listen to, not necessarily fix, a problem. A friend or two is priceless, *but there is a friend who sticks closer than a brother* [or sister].

One of my husband Steve's favorite quotes, "Twenty years from now you will be more disappointed by the things that you didn't do than by the ones you did do. So throw off the bowlines. Sail away from the safe harbor. Explore. Dream. Discover," Mark Twain.

Life is: Good Fragile Precious

- Think through your friends to determine if they are truly reliable (vs. unreliable) Tread cautiously. Guard your heart. *Above all else, guard your heart, for everything you do flows from it* (Proverbs 4:23).
- Think about a friend or family member with whom you can spend valuable time away? Make a list of who and why you would ask them.
- Brainstorm with God and that friend about where you might go to get away.
- Saturate/bathe this escape in prayer prior to leaving your comfort space. Put your prayer down in writing.

Prayer of Encouragement:

Dear Lord, You know what weighs heavily on my mind. Cleanse my mind of worries as my friend and I plan a get together to rejuvenate mind, body, and soul. I desire a clean, fresh slate to absorb Your wisdom and my friend's friendship. Thank you for blessing me with this get away opportunity.

Read meditatively through David's Psalm 104 picturing the power and majesty of God.

Chapter 8

Fearfully and Wonderfully Made

I praise you because I am fearfully and wonderfully made; your works are wonderful, I know that full well. My frame was not hidden from you when I was made in the secret place, when I was woven together in the depths of the earth. Your eyes saw my unformed body; all the days ordained for me were written in your book before one of them came to be—Psalm 139:14–16.

This verse suggests that I should not be complaining, moaning and groaning about the non-working or weak parts of my body. Since I am fearfully and wonderfully made (Scripture says so) and God's works are wonderful, then my body is as it is supposed to be. Every day has been prearranged. God is aware of the exact state of my body yesterday, today, and tomorrow.

I must trust that He knows what He's doing and all is going according to His plan. Simple child-like trust.

"Though the process of aging continues, inwardly you grow stronger with the passing years. Those who live close to Me develop an inner aliveness that makes them seem youthful in spite of their years."[21]

- List your body parts that are working fine.
- How can you turn grumbling into thanking God for what is going well in your life? Give an example as you record your thoughts.
- What are you thankful for in regard to your health? Turn this into a prayer back to God.

Prayer of Encouragement:

Thank you, God, for allowing me a good night's sleep. And thank you for waking me this morning. Please order my steps in this new day that I might be pleasing in Your sight.

Day 36

"To love oneself is the beginning of a life-long romance,"
Oscar Wilde.

I have to ask myself—do I really love myself? Is loving myself selfish, or at best, weird? The correct answer is no. Jesus commands that we *Love your neighbor as yourself*, and sets this as the second most important commandment. The first is this: *Love the Lord your God with all your heart and with all your soul and with all your mind and with all your strength* (Mark 12:28-31).

The verse does not say to love our neighbors MORE than ourselves. So it is then reasonable to conclude that since we are to love our neighbors as much as we love ourselves, we are to love ourselves. Therefore, it is our responsibility to take care of our bodies. Our God-given body, the temple of the Holy Spirit. We are instructed to care for our temples. If I don't take care of me, then who will? If I don't take care of me, how then will I be able to take care of others? (1 Corinthians 6:19–20).

How often do I neglect my own personal need of exercise, fresh air, healthy eating habits, and getting enough sleep? I reason with myself that there is not enough time in the day to study God's Word or to pray. I'm too busy, or too tired. Excuses, excuses. There's always plenty of time for excuses.

Like most people, I busy myself scheduling today, tomorrow, and beyond. If I am to work on the *loving my neighbor as myself* concept, I know it's time to get my life (including my body) in order. My responsibility is to place myself in the healthiest position possible in preparation for surgery and subsequent rehabilitation.

If I really want to fulfill what God desires for me, which is for good and not evil, I must take time for exercise, establish healthy eating habits, and intentional time alone with God. When I commit to those tasks of nurturing my mind, body, and soul, I will be equipped to nurture the souls of others. Then, I can experience the beginning of a true life-long romance, not only with myself, but most importantly with the One who created me.

"Be yourself—not your idea of what you think somebody else's idea of yourself should be," Henry David Thoreau.

- Think about the status of your pantry and refrigerator. What healthy items should you add to your supply of food and snacks? Are there items you should eliminate?
- Where in today's schedule did you pencil in: Appointment with God?
- What new discovery did God reveal to you today? Record your discovery in your journal/notebook.

Day 37

> "Be who you are and say what you mean. Because those who mind don't matter and those who matter don't mind," Dr. Seuss.

This week in the workplace, I detect underlying and outright feelings of anger, passion, greed, and selfishness. When I confronted my boss telling her of my tumor and the need to resign, she did not take the news well. In fact, she put me on a guilt trip stating I would put the organization in a precarious position if I were to leave.

Due to my people-pleasing nature (which can get me in deep trouble), these added negative emotions caused pain, draining my body of stamina. Instead, I must listen to the love song God continually sings to me. *I take great delight in you. I rejoice over you with singing* (Zephaniah 3:17). He takes great delight in me, though others fail and disappoint. He is with me through all time and eternity. "The voices of the world are a cacophony of chaos, pulling you this way and that. Don't listen to those voices; challenge them with My Word. Learn to take minibreaks from the world, finding a place to be still in My Presence and listen to My voice."[22]

I must listen to God's voice and actively seek Him in all I do and say. Since I prayerfully and carefully made the right choice to leave my job, I cannot allow another's viewpoint to cause me to question or alter my decision. God, family, and friends confirm that I need to leave this place of employment and move on. Blessings and peace come as I maintain the decision to depart.

Am I now trying to win the approval of human beings, or of God? Or am I trying to please people? If I were still trying to please people, I would not be a servant of Christ— Galatians 1:10.

- What lessons have you learned along the way regarding other people's reactions to upsetting issues?
- How far are you willing to go to please people; to please God?
- What type of support and encouragement did you receive from family and friends during a challenging time in your life? In what ways was it helpful?

Day 38

God, my God, I yelled for help and you put me together. God, you pulled me out of the grave, gave me another chance at life when I was down-and-out—Psalm 30:2–3/MSG.

Today, I re-started an exercise challenge. I've started and stopped many times, but I am ready to begin again. Why do I stop doing what I know makes me feel better and think more clearly? When I follow through with what I know is best for my body, life is better. Being faithful in exercise before surgery or anytime is wise. My intentions are good. It's the follow through that is lacking. Numerous distractions steer me away from my focus to take care of my body such as:

- People needs and relationship building
- Household tasks (cooking, cleaning, laundry, etc.,)
- Job obligations

I am a work in progress. I do not have this whole in-balance routine figured out yet, but I understand more as I seek God's help and intervention.

"It takes courage to grow up and turn out to be who you really are,"
E. E. Cummings.

- In what area of your life do you feel defeated? Formulate a prayer to God regarding this.
- How will you prevent past downfalls from defeating a new start at a fitness program or other resolution? Record your ideas.
- Who can you ask to be your accountability partner in this area? Pencil in a potential date to contact that individual.

Day 39

Search me, O God, and know my heart; test me and know my anxious thoughts. See if there is any offensive [wicked] way in me, and lead me in the way everlasting— Psalm 139:23-24.

There's no point in pretending with God. He knows my every selfish, evil, and wayward thought before I do. I might be able to fool my family or friends, but no thought or deed gets past the all-knowing Creator of the universe. *You created my inmost being; you knit me together in my mother's womb. I praise you because I am fearfully and wonderfully made; your works are wonderful* (Psalm 139:13-14). How much more involved in my existence could anyone be?

When I returned from a much needed walkabout, I sat down and wrote these words:

Seasons Change

Fall breezes blow briskly
Won't be long now
Rustling leaves of gold and red
Blow hard and land upon green grass

Vibrant yellows, red, and orange mums
Burst forth and say, "Look at me!"
I'm beautiful, alive, and thriving
I have a secret to tell,
Winter's around the corner

Pumpkins soon to be
Nipped by Jack Frost

Day 36-40   *Fearfully and Wonderfully Made*

>   Soon you'll dress in warm garments
>   Won't be long now

As I notice the trees changing in hue every day, I hope and pray I'm changing too, God. Changing to be conformed more like You. Keep me growing and changing to become the person You desire me to be. Becoming better and not bitter. Direction and complete healing come from You.

- Sometimes circumstances blind us. Ask God to point out the error of your ways. Jot down those revelations.
- What thoughts need to be dealt with by the merciful, loving Physician? Share them with God in prayer.
- What proof do you have of His forgiveness?

Day 40

God understands the frail workings of the human body. His son, Jesus, experienced the entire spectrum of emotions including joy, sorrow, grief, pain, and love for all human kind. The poem below illustrates emotions found in Isaiah 53.

Man of Sorrows

He was despised and
Rejected by men
That included me too
Even though I was not there
That fateful day,
That Good Friday

A man of sorrows,
familiar with suffering
the entire world's sin rested
upon His solitary shoulders
that fateful day,
That Good Friday

Carried our sorrows,
considered stricken by God
Though I was not born yet
He knew my propensities
That fateful day
That Good Friday

He was pierced for our transgressions,
crushed for our iniquities
It must be
There is no other way
That fateful day
That Good Friday

The punishment that brought
us peace was upon him
What strange manner of love
To willingly give up all
That fateful day
That Good Friday

By His wounds we are healed
His stripes secured our freedom
Help us remember this day
Our pardon secured
Come Sunday morn
Up from the grave He arose!

God sacrificed so much for me and for each of us. My responsibility is to care for my body. This means to be careful where my body goes, what my body does, and what I ponder. In other words, to be careful what my eyes see, ears hear, tongue says, hands do, feet go, and in whom my heart trusts. Considering

Day 36-40   *Fearfully and Wonderfully Made*

all He has done, is it too much to ask that I keep my body pure and preserved for His glory? To persist in keeping my body unstained by the outside world.

Do you not know that your bodies are temples of the Holy Spirit, who is in you, whom you have received from God? You are not your own; you were bought at a price. Therefore honor God with your bodies—1 Corinthians 6:19–20.

- Consider the treatment and torture Jesus' body endured as you read and meditate on Isaiah 53. Jot down your observations.
- Try to imagine someone righteous suffering for doing good and not opening their mouth in retaliation (Isaiah 53:7). Name some obstacles.
- Take time to pray. Sincerely thank God for sending His Son in order to take away all past, present, and future sins. Write out your prayer.

Prayer of Encouragement:

Oh Lord, You gave Your all that I might have life. Oh, the pain. Oh, the misery You suffered for doing no wrong. I dare not take my fearfully and wonderfully made body for granted. Help me love myself enough to exercise my physical body, as well as, my spiritual mind. Grant me consistency and daily strength. Give me the desire to know You better. Thank you.

Consider the ways God protects, loves, and guides in Psalm 139.

Chapter 9

Strength to the Weary

God sometimes allows our bodies to no longer function normally just to get our attention. Often, that period is for a day or two, but it can be for an extended period. During those conditions, being still and listening to the Holy Spirit's quiet nudging comes more naturally. Otherwise, the din of everyday hectic activity cancels out blessed quiet communion with God.

Are you tired of health-related issues? Weary of financial or relationship stress? Stress can lead to feeling insignificant, useless, and desiring to be anywhere but in our own skin. I've been fighting a cough and cold for too long now. Even the doctor's observation, "There's a lot of that going around," does not help my physical or mental state. I just want her to wave a magic wand over my body bringing instant relief. Discouragement leads to thinking that we will never be well or healed again.

Needing to re-frame my thinking, I choose to accept this waiting period prior to surgery as a gift. A gift of weighing and measuring what is truly important. I am learning what a priority is and what it is not; what I need to dwell upon and what can be set aside for now. One of my mom's favorite Scriptures (and mine too) is tucked inside Isaiah 40, verses 28 through 31:

Do you not know? Have you not heard? The LORD is the everlasting God, the Creator of the ends of the earth. He will not grow tired or weary, and his understanding no one can fathom. He gives strength to the weary and increases the power of the weak. Even youths grow

Day 41-45   *Strength to the Weary*

tired and weary, and young men stumble and fall; but those who hope in the LORD will renew their strength. They will soar on wings like eagles; they will run and not grow weary, they will walk and not be faint.

When our bodies mend, our perspective on life takes on a whole new spin. How quickly we slide back into our normal routine as if we weren't ever down and out. The necessity of slowing our constant motion slips to the back burner. When I get back to normal (whatever that is), I want to remember to say thank you to God and my physicians for restoring me to good health that I normally take for granted.

- Describe the last time you remember complaining.
- What do you feel God might be trying to communicate to you during a wilderness journey?
- During this down-time, what treasures did you take away? Record those riches for future reference.

Prayer of Encouragement:

Father, I place my hope in You, the One who enables me to lift my wings as an eagle. I want to run and not become weary or tired. But, most of all, I want to be all ears to Your voice of guidance. Thank you for this set-aside time to spend resting, healing, and listening. I accept consolation from You. To You, O Lord, I lift up my soul. In You I fully and completely trust.

Day 41

> "Change your perspective and enjoy the adventure. Let the child in you come out and play," Unknown.

The blue swing allowed many children in elementary school to dream big. As soon as the recess bell chimed, I raced to exit the building. When I beat others to a swing, oh what a joyous journey I experienced! The blue swing took me places only my imagination could go. I was no longer in the Bowling Green Elementary School playground in Kentucky. I was magically transported to the ocean, the Grand Canyon, or maybe a castle in England or Ireland. My troubles seemed to magically disappear when this second grader pumped until my short husky legs could pump no more, or when the bell rang, whichever came first. Soaring above reality, I felt free. Airborne, it didn't matter if I received a low math grade. I could not care less whether or not Delores wanted to play with Luanne and not me.

Whenever I spot a swing, my memory returns to mom reciting her favorite poem,

The Swing

Up in the air so blue?
Oh, I do think it the pleasantest thing
Ever a child can do!

Up in the air and over the wall,
Till I can see so wide,
River and trees and cattle and all
Over the countryside—

> Till I look down on the garden green,
> Down on the roof so brown—
> Up in the air I go flying again,
> How do you like to go up in a swing,
> Up in the air and down! [23]

Today, when I think of being transported elsewhere into a spectacular adventure, I think of my long-distance friend. Bonnie and I became buddies while working at the same organization. At that time, both of us were recently married with no children. Now that she's moved away, we strive to get together and communicate as much as possible via email and phone calls. On the top of our priority list is to spend a day perusing thrift shops looking for bargain treasures.

On one infamous trip, I spied two four-foot plastic wise men way up on a high shelf. I never expected to find the exact size and type to match our home outdoor nativity scene. We couldn't suppress our giggles and laughter as we finished shopping. Wonder what other customers thought as they spied our bizarre find: four-foot high plastic wise guys traveling in our shopping carts? Finding just the right size and matching set to our nativity scene—that's another God-thing moment.

When we are together, we walk, talk, walk, and talk some more until we are both hoarse and can talk no more. About then, a hot cup of tea comes in handy. Never having enough time to finish our conversation, but always looking forward to the next time we meet. This is what adventure is all about. Strength attained during the weary stretches.

Teach me your way, LORD, that I may rely on your faithfulness; give me an undivided heart, that I may fear your name— Psalm 86:11.

Life is: Good Fragile Precious

Day 41-45   Strength to the Weary

- Who or what prevents you from doing something just for you today? When can you schedule a renewal activity? (Sometimes just sitting outside or filling a bird feeder, change of scenery and perspective is all it takes to refresh mind, body, and soul—does not have to be far away or involve a long amount of time).
- What is your definition of an undivided heart?
- How might you go about achieving an undivided heart? Journal your thoughts.

Day 42

"Fresh air and exercise: the best medicine in the world," stated my doctor. I'm having a hard time staying positive. I would like to be eager and anticipate my upcoming birthday, but it's not working. The day is overcast and grey, not unlike my attitude.

Trying to talk myself into the notion that tomorrow will be better, I debated with myself whether or not to exercise. I decided to lace up my tennis shoes and head in the direction of a nearby small creek. *Should I turn around or keep going? If I could just reach my favorite spot and linger over the bridge*, I prayed. Calm waters remind me of the words in Psalm 42, *As the deer pants for streams of water, so my soul pants for you, O God. My soul thirsts for God, for the living God. When can I go and meet with God?*

Pushing myself to go a bit further, I rounded the corner and saw the flash of a white tail. They saw me. We all froze in our tracks. About 150 feet away stood two deer pausing to quench their thirst. An affirmation and reward appeared that morning in the form of God's majestic creatures—almost as if God were saying, "I'm glad you took the time to seek me out."

- In what way(s) can you pant for God as a deer pants for water?
- Goal for today: walk in the amazing outdoors. Write a prayer about what you sensed (saw, heard, smelled) on this walk thanking God for giving you His strength and ambition to accomplish this goal.
- List two blessings or rewards received after choosing to exercise and renew your energy.

Day 43

The Shepherd [said], "Dare to begin to be happy. If you will go forward in the way before you, you will soon receive the promise, and I will give you your heart's desire," Hannah Hurnard.

Questions fill my head. *Will I be found faithful?* I want to glorify God in all that I do and say. Am I truly making the most of every opportunity?

My hair stylist Jim arranged my hair so that when my left side gets shaved for surgery, I'll still have some hair to cover the stitches. Afterwards, he gave me a big bear hug and said everything was going to be fine. Bless his heart.

Will these be my final days? I wonder if this will be my last birthday celebration. Family and friends shower me with birthday songs and greetings, lunches, dinners, emails, and gifts. My Bible study ladies pray for me by name and others commit to pray for a good surgery outcome. I feel loved and supported. I am loved by many. Either way, I know the story ends well. Whether I return to my earthly home and recover, or go live with my Father in heaven forever.

For I fully expect and hope that I will never be ashamed, but that I will continue to be bold for Christ, as I have been in the past. And I trust that my life will bring honor to Christ, whether I live or die— Philippians 1:20/NLT.

- Remembering your last celebration, in what way(s) did this uplift your countenance and attitude?
- What do you think it means to be bold for Christ? Do you feel you are bold for Him? If so, record those ways you go about being bold.
- Think of someone who could use a thinking of you note. Set aside a few minutes to jot down encouraging words to this person.

Day 44

Jesus replied, Anyone who drinks this water will soon become thirsty again. But those who drink the water I give will never be thirsty again. It becomes a fresh, bubbling spring within them, giving them eternal life.
Please, sir, the woman said, give me this water! Then I'll never be thirsty again, and I won't have to come here to get water—John 4:13–15/NLT.

I walk in the rain with an umbrella. The walk feels good to my weary body. I'm 80 percent relaxed and 20 percent not relaxed. The need to get stuff done takes precedence over my need to be mindful of Him. It feels like there are more people to see/meet/interact with than hours in my day. My energy's gone before the day is done. I must remember to be content in my own skin and not compare my energy level to someone else's reservoir.

The rain pours reminding me of the living water our women's Bible study group discussed. Jesus asks a Samaritan woman to give him a drink from the well. The woman was shocked that a man might ask a woman—and a Samaritan woman at that. Normally, Jews did not associate with Samaritans. Jesus tells us that if we drink of this living water, we will never thirst again.

- Thirsting after God: what does that concept mean to you? Have you ever thirsted after God? What did you do to quench that thirst? Use those thoughts to write a love letter to God.
- What is your heart's desire?
- How can you be certain that you possess eternal life? Would a friend/neighbor find enough evidence to label you a Christian/follower of the Lord Jesus Christ?

Day 45

This is the day the Lord has made; let us rejoice and be glad in it—Psalm 118:24.

My dear husband, Steve, surprised me with a weekend getaway for my birthday. We rode our motorcycle north on a color tour through glorious changing fall leaves. Together, we waited from our balcony swing for the pizza delivery. The sunset touched the tips of maple trees just beginning to show hints of oranges and reds. What a privilege to participate in God's wonder displayed right before our eyes.

After hungrily devouring the food, I immersed myself in a book while he took photographs. When it became too dark, Steve moved the motel's floor lamp outside to the balcony so I could read. He continued to experiment with different light settings and lenses to capture various effects looking out at the lighthouse and pier.

Will this be the last year to see God's majestic creation as the season changes? Worry uses precious energy and leaves a body drained and unable to cope or make wise decisions. When a worry pops up, this can be a reminder to pray.

Day 41-45 *Strength to the Weary*

- In what way do you trust God with this day, with your life?
- Name three things you can be thankful for and rejoice over.
- Describe the last time you felt God's renewed strength flow through you? Create a prayer thanking God for this gift.

Prayer of Encouragement:

Dear God, thank you for showing me the wonder and beauty of Your majesty through the season changes. I am learning the more I focus on You, the stronger my strength grows. When I sense my energy fading, I'll look to You; my ultimate source of strength.

Read through Isaiah 40. Choose a few favorite words or phrases that speak comfort to you.

Chapter 10

Years Fly Swiftly Away

The length of our days is seventy years—or eighty, if we have the strength; yet their span is but trouble and sorrow, for they quickly pass, and we fly away—Psalm 90:10.

"Hi, Teresa, I just wanted to tell you … my daddy died this morning. He was riding his bicycle and the Lord took him home with a massive heart attack. I wanted you to know my mother is alone now."

I replayed the telephone message over and over again to make sure I'd heard it correctly. My dear friend Bonnie fought to hold the tears back. I felt her intense pain and the effort it took to verbalize those words. Our history goes back BK (before kids) spanning over 30 years. She now lives in another state, and we continue to visit each other as often as possible. Together, we survived work-related issues, teen uprisings, graduations, and weddings.

I recall with fond memories one of our visits to her Pennsylvania hometown. My husband and I stayed overnight in her parent's home because Bonnie and her husband were in the process of building their new house. We made the journey to Pennsylvania just weeks after our baby number two, Amanda, was born. While supposedly napping, our baby number one son, Andrew (just over a year old) tried to escape through their second floor screened window. Miraculously, Bonnie's brother spied an arm and leg hanging out the window *before* our ingenious child landed on the garage roof. Even though his given name is Andrew, we nicknamed him Little Houdini.

Over the years, Bonnie's folks Milton and Dolly graciously offered their second floor apartment to friends and family. Hospitality came naturally for our Pennsylvania "parents," and we always felt like family in their presence.

Milton died just the way he would have wanted: healthy and doing what he enjoyed. When I heard Bonnie's shaky words on the telephone, my mind immediately went to my own father. The same unpredictable event could happen any day to my father. Reality struck me—I need to strive to keep in touch with him. I picked up the phone and called my dad.

- Is there someone with whom you need to be spending more time with on a regular basis? What plans can you make to accomplish this?
- Who can you think of that you need to forgive? What steps do you need to take toward the road to forgiveness?
- To whom do you need to say, I love you and genuinely mean it? Maybe it's time to make that phone call or visit.

Prayer of Encouragement:

Father, thank you for loving me even when I'm often unlovable. Help me see other people through Your eyes. If there is someone I need to speak to or visit, please make it clear to me so I will not miss an opportunity to show Christ to them. My desire is to be present today with those You have placed in my path and not to worry about tomorrow's troubles.

Day 46

My voice enthusiastically sings along with this song I recently heard, *Sing to the King* (lyrics by Billy Foote):

> Come, let us sing a song
>
> A song declaring, we belong to Jesus
>
> He's all we need
>
> Lift up a heart of praise
>
> Sing now with voices raised to Jesus
>
> Sing to the king
>
> Come, let us sing a song

I began the day in tears. I miss my dear mom. Every Mother's Day after she died is not an easy day. If I chose one word to describe her, it would be encourager. My biggest cheerleader. If I stretch my imagination, I can see her waving imaginary pom-poms and saying, *You go, girl. I knew you could do it. I'm proud of you!* She'd be ecstatic about my published articles and books, and so sorrowful about me having to undergo brain surgery. Loving on her grandchildren and great-grandchildren would bring pure joy.

Even today, certain sights, sounds, and smells evoke memories of our dear mom. For instance, I cannot taste or see a lemon bar (listed under Recipes at back of book) without thinking of her. Lemon bars still remain a favorite to eat and prepare, along with Chocolate Miracle Whip Cake, etc. As I bake these delightful recipes, my mind and heart returns to mom. While walking or driving with my children or grandchildren, I try naming various flowers and trees mom taught me. This eases the pain somewhat, however the painful loss never really disappears.

How could my mom, a good woman, wife, mother, grandmother, sister, and daughter be taken from us at such a young age? I do not have the answer to that question. God chose to bring her home to Heaven and to Him. Yet, deep down I realize that God's *thoughts are not your thoughts, neither are your ways my ways* (Isaiah 55:8).

Even though I experience rough times remembering my dear, sweet mom, I felt blessed beyond measure by the end of the day. God is indeed awesome! From tears of sorrow to tears of joy. He redeemed my sorrowful heart and showed me wealth and beauty all around. I needed to search diligently and open my eyes. God filled in the gaps of missing mom with love and generosity in creative ways on that Mother's Day:

1. Amanda, our daughter, came bearing thoughtful gifts. Just her physical appearance brought instant joy.
2. Andrew, our son, and his wife Bethany and children called from Minnesota to wish me Happy Mother's Day. Plus, they sent beautiful flowers with a lovingly hand-crafted card and bookmark.
3. Steve's mother came over. The four of us enjoyed a picnic on the deck under beautiful sunny skies. Chef Steve grilled yummy steaks and asparagus.
4. We three women enjoyed chat time on the patio swing.

Life is: Good Fragile Precious

5. Later, Amanda, Steve, and I toured on our motorcycles up north and walked around Long Lake Park. My two photography geeks took photos of spring bursting forth. New fond memories made that day.

"And it isn't the thing you do, dear. It's the thing you leave undone which gives you a bit of a heartache at the setting of the sun,"
Margaret Sangster.

- What causes sorrow in your heart? Name those trigger points.
- What evokes feelings of joy in you? List those positive feelings also.
- Where or how do you find joy during a celebration time such as Mother's/Father's Day, or a birthday? Journal some past joyous occasions. Look back on these uplifting revelations during low seasons.

Day 47

Teach us to realize the brevity of life, so that we may grow in wisdom—
Psalm 90:12/NLT.

After a visit to the dentist, I drove through the old neighborhood. I do this several times a year when I'm in the mood to travel down Memory Lane. The dentist office is the same one I visited when we first moved to Michigan during my high school years. My dentist of over twenty years recently retired, and then died after a short struggle with Parkinson's disease.

I remember looking out my bedroom window at a tree that burst forth with pink blossoms. The new occupants significantly changed the entrance and garden area. No more rose bushes. I can almost see mom out there on her knees trimming the multicolored rose bushes—her pride and joy. We'd often see her handiwork cut and in a vase on the kitchen counter for all to enjoy their beauty and fragrance.

Just down the road from where my folks built our house, a community center still stands. The center included a pool, tennis courts, playground, and ball diamond. Parking near the community center, I remained fixed in time longing to bring back fond memories. I placed a blanket on the ground with my journal and pencil. Allowing the scene to soak into my mind and heart, I wrote these words:

Time Moves On and So Must I
Building still stands
With few improvements
Swimming pool where I took lessons

Tennis courts complete with grass stubble
Where boyfriend (now husband) & I
Lobbed balls in the hot sun

Swings and slide
Where my children played
While visiting Grandma and Grandpa

Circle of Life
Bodies grow older
Wrinkles, aches, and weight increase

Life is: Good Fragile Precious

Those were the days
Thoughts of hardship
Crossed my mind

Yet, little did I know
Those were carefree, happier times
Age and health not an issue then

Like to think
I'm still me
Deep inside this aging vessel

Like to think
I could still play tennis
And swing high above the treetops
If I wanted to, I could

Teach us to number our days, that we may gain a heart of wisdom—Psalm 90:12/NIV.

- Recall a past memory and thank God for it.
- What intentional steps are you taking to live wisely and well these days? Name those steps.
- List the ways in which you see yourself growing wiser day by day.

Day 48

But our citizenship is in heaven. And we eagerly await a Savior from there, the Lord Jesus Christ, who, by the power that enables him to bring everything under his control, will transform our lowly bodies so that they will be like his glorious body—
Philippians 3:20-21.

On Thursday, the television aired news of a house fire that consumed an entire family. I was shocked to learn one of the victims was a co-worker. She, her husband, and their 15-year old daughter all died in the fire. On Tuesday, I had spoken to her at work; on Wednesday, she was gone. The same day, a dear friend of mine told me her 95-year old grandfather took his last breath on this earth. The family felt comfort in the fact that at age 83, he accepted the Lord as his personal Savior. The deaths of the family, I would classify as unnatural; the second death of my friend's grandfather—natural.

Life is about change. Some deaths I do not understand, such as a whole family being wiped out from a house fire. Other changes like death of a loved one, I find hard to accept. As I interact with family and friends, I realize I will not reside here on earth forever. I do not have the luxury of wasting days. When I am wrong, I need to be swift to apologize. Taking every opportunity to tell and show others that I love them. Sharing what God is teaching me through the heartaches and miracles.

I regularly attend a local writers' group chapter of Word Weavers International. Their vision is threefold—community, critique, and conference. A fellow member of Word Weavers, Loyd Boldman, recently went home to heaven's glory. Loyd, a creative artist, writer, and singer blessed with stupendous talent and professional integrity now sings before the King of Kings. None of us can count on tomorrow. This great gift of today God has given you … use it to the fullest. Use it to honor God. Loyd sang the words to this song:

> *"O Jah, Let God arise! O Jah, Let God arise! Extol Him that rideth upon the Heavens—By His name Yahweh, let's rejoice before Him."*

- What fond memories are you making right now? Which ones would you like to be creating? Talk to God about your thoughts and dreams.
- How might you recognize seeds of bitterness in your heart? Prayerfully communicate those thoughts to God.
- What preparation can you make for citizenship in heaven? Jot down any notes.

Day 49

> *"I believe in Christ like I believe in the sun—not because I can see it, but by it I can see everything else,"* C.S. Lewis.

Senator Edward Kennedy was diagnosed with a malignant brain tumor. He died from brain cancer the following year. This shocking news came less than a week after my own brain tumor diagnosis. Hearing about Kennedy's much publicized death; I cannot help but wonder about my own outcome. No one knows how long the tumor's grown there. Mine could be cancerous even though the doctors suspect it to be benign. Kennedy's tumor proved cancerous and fatal. Family members, extended family, and friends are in mourning after Kennedy's death. Regardless of political beliefs, he was a human being: A son, brother, husband, father, uncle, and grandfather.

Day 46-50   *Years Fly Swiftly Away*

It is difficult not to compare his end result with my own. *Will God choose for me to live? Why does He choose some to live and others to die?* I do not know my end result, but God does. Life is fragile and precious. None of us know from one day to the next if we will still be walking and talking on planet earth. Some will live longer on planet earth than others, but in the end, we are all terminal. Each day needs to count. Others need to know the hope that resides inside my heart.

"Our great Shepherd takes us to Himself tenderly and personally, granting us times of joy in His nearer presence. There He nourishes us one-on-one as if we're the only sheep in His flock," Tim Truorpen.

- Name a few things you did today that will count for eternity. Are you satisfied with the list? Talk to God about the results.
- Do you feel God shaping you to live in the present? If so, list the ways you feel this is happening.
- In what way(s) did you exercise your faith in the last seven days?

Day 50

A reminder from Apostle Paul helps put trying circumstances into perspective, *My grace is sufficient for you, for my power is made perfect in weakness ... That is why, for Christ's sake, I delight in weaknesses, in insults, in hardships, in persecutions, in difficulties. For when I am weak, then I am strong*—2 Corinthians 12:9–10.

Why in the world would I want to get out of bed early on a Saturday? Not only that, but the day is cold and windy. I could remain in a perfectly warm bed. Weeks ago, my friend asked if I would walk with her in the Susan G.

Komen Race for the Cure. Proceeds from the walk help fight breast cancer. My friend is a breast cancer survivor. How could I say no? In fact, five of my friends survived breast cancer—four in just the last year, and one is a 10-year survivor!

Still, I wrestle with wrangling myself from my cozy domain. All the doubts escape me when I near the mall area. Over 7,000 participants gather. Local merchants donate coffee, bagels, yogurt and the like. It takes many volunteers to pull off such an enormous, profitable event. Collections totaled nearly $500,000 just in our area.

I can't help but notice all the pink registration numbers. Pink signals the individual is a breast cancer survivor. One group wears a t-shirt with a name of a young girl's birth and death dates. The mother proudly displays her celebration, my daughter and I— meaning the daughter died of breast cancer, and the mother is a survivor. Another male wears a sign stating, "I race in celebration of my wife Traci. I walk beside her today so that I don't need to walk without her tomorrow." Wow, it's hard to hold back tears as I read the numerous signs around me. Sign after sign folks declare their love, celebration, and pain as name after name is written in display on their backs.

I am not in control of my destiny. It is still important to take care of my body as best as I'm able to today, such as eating properly, getting exercise and sufficient rest. But when it comes right down to it, if God sees fit that today is my last day on earth, today will be my last day on earth. No ifs, ands, or buts about it. I am the first to admit I do not treasure every day, or every moment as I should. My mind is usually so far ahead of this particular moment that I miss present blessings. But I am learning.

> "Grief never ends … but it changes. It's a passage, not a place to stay. Grief is not a sign of weakness, nor a lack of faith … it is the price of love," Unknown.

Day 46-50   *Years Fly Swiftly Away*

- Think about a time when a hardship or struggle affected you, and how you handled the situation.
- Pray to God about how you plan to enjoy today, right here, and right now. A good tip to remember, "Years may wrinkle the skin, but to give up interest wrinkles the soul."[24]
- What heavenly treasures are you storing up? Are there earthly or heavenly ones in your stockpile? Meditate and compare the two types of treasures.

Prayer of Encouragement:

Dear God, when I rush from one event to the next, I am never fully engaged or present at either location. Speak peace to me so I will not worry about things You are handling. I want to rest in You and allow You to be my strong anchor in the midst of a storm.

How many character qualities of God you can find in Psalm 90? Consider how those traits stir you.

Chapter 11

Had Your Nap Today?

Elijah was afraid and ran for his life. When he came to Beersheba in Judah, he left his servant there, while he himself went a day's journey into the wilderness. He came to a broom bush, sat down under it and prayed that he might die. I have had enough, Lord, he said. Take my life; I am no better than my ancestors. Then he lay down under the bush and fell asleep. All at once an angel touched him and said, Get up and eat. He looked around, and there by his head was some bread baked over hot coals, and a jar of water. He ate and drank and then lay down again.

The angel of the Lord came back a second time and touched him and said, Get up and eat, for the journey is too much for you. So he got up and ate and drank. Strengthened by that food, he traveled forty days and forty nights until he reached Horeb, the mountain of God— 1 Kings 19:3–8.

Weary Elijah fled from those who wanted him dead. Depressed, desperate, and feeling alone, he lacked emotional and physical strength to continue on his journey. I imagine he felt giving up would be easier. God allowed Elijah to sleep, and then lovingly sent an angel bringing food and drink. God assured Elijah, *I reserve seven thousand in Israel—all whose knees have not bowed down to Baal.* Elijah was not alone. Many others still followed God. Due to Elijah's exhaustion, he was not thinking clearly. God would not abandon Elijah. He felt as though God had abandoned him, but quite the contrary. This set

Day 51-55   Had Your Nap Today?

apart time proved vital to assess, evaluate and re-group. Similar to hitting the pause button to replenish mental and physical fatigue.

"When the brain is idle and disengaged from external stimuli, we can finally tap into our inner stream of thoughts, emotions, memories and ideas. Engaging this network helps us to make meaning out of our experiences, empathize with others, be more creative and reflect on our own mental and emotional states."[25]

Wondering when the testing ends: EKG, flu shot, blood lab work, stress tests, etc. This must be how lab rats feel. Even though it is necessary to make sure I am healthy enough for surgery, the poking, procedures, and testing exhausts me.

Perhaps there is something that confuses you, draining your emotional and physical strength. Maybe it's a health issue or money problem. Possibly, a relationship is not working out the way you had hoped. I empathize with your concern for someone you love who currently serves our country or a returning veteran.

God provides a prescription for discouragement. He does not confuse physical weariness with spiritual weakness. After Elijah rested, ate bread, drank water, he was ready for service. He was then in a more stable condition to receive needed insight about his next move. God can do the same for you and me if we don't fill in the blank spaces.

"When God brings blank space, don't fill it in!"—Oswald Chambers.

- How many hours of sleep do you need to function efficiently? Are you getting enough sleep? If not, consider putting sleep at the top of your priority list.
- When did you last feel weary and overwhelmed? Be still and reflect on how God took care of you in that situation. Journal your thoughts.
- Slow down; even if only for five minutes. Walk away from and turn off all electronics. Take a few deep breaths, inhale and exhale slowly. Ask God to show you your next move after a rest period.

Prayer of Encouragement:

Dear God, forgive me for rushing through a day without much thought of You and Your love. I realize not all questions will receive a response. In Your perfect timeframe and in Your way, You take care of these matters. Thank you for being patient. I am thankful you care about me enough to lead the way through this confusing maze.

Day 51

Let the beloved of the Lord rest secure in Him, for He shields him all day long, and the one the Lord loves rests between His shoulders—Deuteronomy 33:12.

The National Sleep Foundation[26] suggests six reasons why I need to fight for a better night's rest. It makes sense that when I do not sleep well I'm susceptible to sickness and stress which can lead to making unwise decisions.

Day 51-55   *Had Your Nap Today?*

1. Sleep helps maintain a strong immune system. Depriving oneself of sleep compromises immune function and makes a body more vulnerable to disease.

2. Sleep slows aging. Too little sleep elevates levels of stress hormones and lowers levels of growth hormone necessary for cell repair. In one study, young, healthy sleep-deprived subjects had the hormonal profiles of much older people.

3. Sleeplessness increases insulin resistance, a precursor to type 2 diabetes. Guarding the proper amount of sleep in your body can prevent diabetes.

4. Proper amount of sleep helps keeps you slim. When you are sleep deprived, you have more of the appetite-stimulating hormone ghrelin in your blood and less appetite-curbing leptin, a combo that leaves you longing for junk food.

5. Sleep helps maintain a sharp memory. Even one sleepless night impairs concentration and memory and can affect job performance.

6. Sleep can make you happier. Insomniacs face a higher risk of depression, alcoholism, and suicide.

God is the Giver of all good and perfect gifts. From His gracious hand, I accept the gift of rest, life, and sunshine. Jesus is the Lover of my soul. As I nestle beneath a warm blanket, I pencil these words in my journal:

Hidden Treasure

Part of the day all mine
A treasure—
nugget of gold
Handed me in the form of a
Ray of morning sunlight
Warms my cheek
And my soul

This day is a gift
A priceless one
Let me not waste
Nor squander

Clinging to
Peace
Comfort
Tranquility

- Record how you felt and functioned after resting the needed amount of hours. Contrast that with a sleep-deprived day.
- What did the Lord teach you during a quiet period this week?
- During the last week or months, have you learned a truth you could share with someone verbally or in written form? Is there a belief you need to change? A behavior to adjust?

Day 52

He will not let you stumble; the one who watches over you will not slumber. Indeed, he who watches over Israel never slumbers or sleeps—Psalm 121:3–4.

Psalm 121 is called the Traveler's Psalm. Pilgrims travel many miles through lonely country in order to reach their destination. The days and nights can be long and wearisome. Knowing they are protected by the Maker of heaven and earth pacifies the soul and allows blessed, necessary rest.

"Naps make you smarter and boost your ability to learn," according to researchers at the University of California, Berkley.[27] The longer we stay awake, the less able our brains are to learn. "Just 60 minutes of shut-eye can boost learning ability significantly ... Sleep clears the brain's short-term memory storage to make room for new learning." It stands to reason I should periodically take time out for some shut-eye. Since the God who cares for me never sleeps, why should both of us stay awake? He's always on the job: watching, protecting, and loving.

As we age, it becomes more impossible to fall asleep and then to sleep peacefully for an extended period of time. Try a routine with no connectivity to electronic devices an hour before bedtime. The ever-advancing technology in our time needs to be used with caution and care. There are other safer, healthier ways to feel relaxed and capture a sense of release.

> "I personally love meditating as I lay down to go to sleep, or you can try playing some music as you drift off to sleep, or even listening to an audiobook or guided meditation."[28]

Light, positive reading prior to bedtime (avoiding action-packed, negative material) can aid in restful slumber. Choose a spiritual thought, Bible verse, or prayer to focus on. Fixing your mind on those reflections help deflect random mind wanderings. Jesus is my righteousness, and I stand complete in Him. If insomnia persists (which is common), talk this over with a physician willing to work with you.

"Let's begin by taking a smallish nap or two," Winnie the Pooh.

- What or who stands in the way of your getting the proper amount of sleep in order to function at your prime? List your sleep inhibitors.
- Have you come to the point that you acknowledged it is not selfish to nap if you are feeling tired? If so, good for you! It took me many years before I came to that realization. Journal how you plan to prepare your body and mind prior to laying down to rest.
- Take a few minutes and formulate a thank-you prayer to God for uninterrupted, blessed rest. *In peace I will lie down and sleep, for you alone, Lord, make me dwell in safety* (Psalm 4:8).

Day 53

I look up to the mountains—does my help come from there? My help comes from the Lord, who made heaven and earth! He will not let you stumble; the one who watches over you will not slumber. Indeed, he who watches over Israel never slumbers or sleeps. The Lord himself watches over you! The Lord stands beside you as your protective shade. The sun will not harm you by day, nor the moon at night—Psalm 121:1–8/NLT.

Negative feelings, be gone! I choose to have no part in the woe is me zone. I choose positive, happy, uplifting thoughts. Last evening my friend and

Day 51-55   *Had Your Nap Today?*

I shared a wonderful atmosphere with delicious food and companionship. Speaking our minds. Being genuine. We often remind each other to, let go and let God—giving Him control over my life including surgery details and beyond.

Tonight I'm meeting my daughter Amanda at a local pottery shop. I plan to paint Christmas ornaments; she has chosen a pink pig. I have not attempted to paint pottery before, so I am eager to learn. Laughing at our mistakes and creative tries, we enjoy a grand serendipitous time. I love this chance for us to unwind together, to be spontaneous and alive with no agenda! I feel at ease and thankful to share time with my daughter-friend.

By the end of the week, I do not have much energy left. Motivation is slim. My brain operates on overload. Part of me says to rest and take it easy. Knowing my home will not be organized in the few weeks before surgery, emotions take their toll. I sense God telling me, *Rest child, your journey ahead demands all you possess and more.*

> "Taking naps sounds so childish. I prefer to call them horizontal life pauses," Unknown.

- Do you feel as if God disappointed you at some time(s) or in some way? If so, describe the details surrounding this occurrence. Can you see a glimpse of what God was doing back then?
- What (if any) negative thoughts do you still harbor due to the disappointment? Record those thoughts and offer them up to God.
- Name an incident(s) when God stood beside you through a particularly rocky time. Recall God's blessings of protection from harm. Journal a prayer of thankfulness to God for keeping watch over you.

Life is: Good Fragile Precious

Day 54

> Silly cat!
>
> Chases her tail
>
> Round and round she goes
>
> Katie, silly cat!
>
> Don't you know
>
> Just how silly you look
>
> Twirling around
>
> Aimlessly
>
> Vigorously
>
> Plops herself down
>
> Within a patch of sun
>
> As if to declare,
>
> I'm worn out
>
> Time for a nap!

It's quite humorous watching our tabby cat chase her own tail. After moving wildly about, she'll plop down in sheer exhaustion. I thought about how I, too, should be napping. Other times both cats will chase each other round and round the house, up and down the steps, then curl up beside each other. Tabby and Siamese cats play together. They seem to forget the skirmish just minutes before. When they're tired, they stretch out (often in the sun) and rest. Later, without warning, they're ready to tackle another feat. Maybe human beings should imitate cats.

Today, my doctor ordered a treadmill stress test. They would like me to endure for as long as possible. Seven to eight minutes would be a valid test. I made it to ten minutes without falling off and injuring myself! Both the cardiologist and my family doctor say I passed. So, we're good to go for surgery.

Day 51-55   Had Your Nap Today?

A surgery date has been finalized, confirmed, and placed on multiple calendars. Just the thought of an official date feels definitive and scary. The only way to make the tumor and extra bone growth go away is through major surgery. No turning back.

Our task as followers of God is to bravely accept God's grace. With confidence we can endure affliction and uncertainty with patience. I must *Wait for the Lord; be strong and take heart and wait for the Lord* (Psalm 27:14).

> "Sometimes the most urgent thing you can possibly do is to take a complete rest," Ashleigh Brilliant.

- How easy is it for you to wait? On a scale of 1-5 (5 being the most patient; 1 being the least patient), where do you stand on the patience scale? Record your insights and review them the next time you find yourself waiting for something or someone.
- Can you be strong and courageous as you wait for God's perfect timing? If so, what is the plan to accomplish this task?
- Notice in Psalm 27:14 the words *Wait for the Lord* appears two times—once at the beginning and again at the end. What do you suppose is the significance of this repetition?

Day 55

You have six days when you can do your work, but the seventh day of each week belongs to me, your God ... In six days I made the sky, the earth, the oceans, and everything in them, but on the seventh day I rested. That's why I made the Sabbath a special day that belongs to me—Exodus 20:9–11/CEV.

Moses told the Israelites what the Lord had said, Every generation of Israelites must respect the Sabbath. This day will always serve as a reminder, both to me and to the Israelites, that I made the heavens and the earth in six days, then on the seventh day I rested and relaxed—Exodus 31:16–17/CEV.

This fourth commandment, *Remember the Sabbath day by keeping it holy* (Exodus 20:8) is a reminder to God's people of their freedom from previous slavery in Egypt. Granted, we do not live in the time period when God gave the 10 commandments to the Israelites, but we can benefit by following the commandments as closely as possible. The Sabbath is a sacred day, one on which to remember the ultimate sacrifice God made. He allowed His only Son to die on the cross for our sin and rose again the third day. This proved He is who He claimed to be. The Almighty God has ultimate power over life and death.

Do you set aside time each week to honor Sabbath-rest? How would honoring God look in your busy life? Some may opt to fast and pray. Others deliberately unplug from technology—the goal being to unplug and remove self from anything or anyone distracting. Walk away from things and move closer to God. Deliberate feasting on God's Word, and in prayer, is **never** wasted time. You may choose an evening, morning, or day of the week. Here are a few suggested activities during Sabbath-rest time:

Day 51-55 Had Your Nap Today?

1. Gather with others in assembly worship of Almighty God.
2. Sing praises to God. Lift heart and hands to the Giver and Sustainer of life and breath.
3. Pray and share blessings and answered prayer with one another. One method of prayer is the **ACTS** formula: beginning with **A**doration, then **C**onfession, **T**hanksgiving, and ending with **S**upplication (ask or petition).
4. Ponder on God's bountiful gifts. Refresh your mind with past journal entries.
5. Rest up for the week ahead.

"In our leisure we reveal what kind of people we are," Ovid.

- How were you rewarded by attending a worship service this week?
- Name a song(s) that helps you remember God's gifts and unconditional love. Write out the lyrics to the song and keep it handy for future reference. Lift your voice heavenward and sing to the King of Kings (it doesn't matter how musically talented you are or are not).
- What portion of your busy schedule will you devote to honor a Sabbath-rest? Make a reminder note in your calendar and keep the date.

Extra Credit: take the time to check out the song, *10,000 Reasons/Bless the Lord*, by Matt Redman. Whenever I sing the words, *Bless the Lord O my soul, worship His holy name, Sing like never before* …, I get tingly chills all over feeling warm encouragement and closeness to the only wise God.

Prayer of Encouragement:

Dear God, I praise You for protection and guidance in the right direction. Help me remember that You made the Sabbath for human beings, not human beings for the Sabbath. My desire is to do Your will in Your way. I place my agenda, life, and the lives of my loved ones in capable hands as I comfortably rest in You.

Meditate on these comforting words expressed in Psalm 4:8. What do those words mean to you personally—*I will both lie down in peace, and sleep; for You alone, O Lord, make me dwell in safety.*

Life is: Good Fragile Precious

Chapter 12

Slip Away

"Some people drain you and others provide soul food. Get in the company of those who feed your spirit," Thema Davis.

As I step into a friend's house, I'm thankful there are still a few places I can go to relax and be myself. Especially since I cannot go back to mom and dad's house anymore. This emotion is complicated to describe other than it is right and safe, and I do not desire to be anywhere else on earth at that moment in time. The physical house still exists, but my mom does not—at least not here on earth.

This is rare for me. Most places I need to consciously remind myself to be present, and not think forward or be apprehensive. When I project myself into the future, I miss blessings of the moment. I know this happens, yet it takes great effort to not pre-plan or think backward of what could or should have been. Those thoughts rob me of today's joy. There's no need to think ahead of what I need to do next or where I need to go, or about any other appointments. I just am. Present in the moment. Totally comfortable helping myself to something to eat or drink. The furniture's right. Not too firm or too soft. The atmosphere and environment is such that I can say or do anything without feeling guilty.

I wonder if this is what heaven will be like, only better. No more tears or sorrow in heaven. Joy everlasting and peace all the time. No longing to be

Day 56-60 Slip Away

anywhere else or with anyone else because God's presence will fill every desire; a picture incomprehensible to imagine.

My final destination is far better than I can ever dream. I find temporary solace in rare locations such as my friend's cabin, camper, mattress on the floor of a mobile home porch, or conference grounds bunk bed. Imagine a permanent location where there's no medical/financial stress, burdens, or pain. Makes you desire that mansion-home even more, doesn't it? As much as it pains me to think about an unfavorable outcome from surgery, I can rejoice knowing God's already done the prep work for my mansion-home in Heaven. As Pastor Jim says, "It's going to turn out all right."

Do not let your hearts be troubled. You believe in God; believe also in me. My Father's house has many rooms; if that were not so, would I have told you that I am going there to prepare a place for you? And if I go and prepare a place for you, I will come back and take you to be with me that you also may be where I am. You know the way to the place where I am going— John 14:1–4.

- Close your eyes. Picture in your mind living in a future perfect place that God designed for you. Describe the environment of this place.
- What might this place look like? Read Revelation 21, 22:1–5.
- What part of heaven, the New Jerusalem—Holy City, will you look forward to most? Why?

Prayer of Encouragement:

Dear God, thank you for being the ultimate planner and soul food provider. I can come to You anytime day or night with a concern. I'm thankful for the family you placed me in and friends who care and pray for my physical and emotional well-being. Amen.

Day 56

Below is a poem I created after a Sister-Friends Forever luncheon:

> **Circle of Friends**
>
> Friends come and go
> Others stick around
> Like a comfortable pair of shoes
> Or a well-worn favorite nightgown
>
> Today, we meet again
> Break bread together
> Heart beats a bit faster
> Pulse races a little quicker
>
> Feeling joy
> Hugs all around
> Smiles abound
>
> Sharing hearts
> About our children,
> Grandchildren and spouses
> Caring. Listening. Affirming
>
> Lasting friendships
> Such a treasure-gift
> Something money cannot buy

Day 56-60 *Slip Away*

> One in the spirit
> Sister connections
> One with the Lord

Personal spiritual recharge and interaction with others are two vital ingredients. Consistent embracing of these life enhancements goes a long way toward promoting a healthy love for self and neighbor. We need each other. Joy comes when we consistently give and receive refreshment from friends and family. I just completed a captivating and stick-with-you book entitled, *The Blue Zones, 9 lessons for living longer from the people who've lived the longest.*[29] More about this book in the back section under Good Reads.

Friends advise that time apart from spouse, family, and regular routines can be valuable. Time to rejuvenate, inspire, and encourage. We need a friend or two who pick us up when the rest of the world appears gloomy, depressed, and only wants to kick us while we're down.

- Who in your life do you feel comfortable to go to in times of stress or joy?
- If you don't have someone like this on your favorites list, try looking around to find someone. Pause now and pray, asking God to help you find that special person.
- Name a few positive aspects of your life that you can share with this individual. Feel free to confide in them when you struggle with a certain feeling/issue.

Day 57

> "The person who can bring the spirit of laughter into a room is indeed blessed," Bennett Cerf.

Our feet soaked in lavender smelling salts. Each gal scrubbed her face and moisturized with soft crème. What a relaxing, unwinding time to just be. I was able to bond with my friend and meet new people interested in my writing and brain surgery path. True friends remind me when it is time to cease work activities and make time to chill and have fun. Free to share similar journeys of tiredness and frustration struggles. Our common denominator: continually doing for others; everyone except self.

While deciding what to purchase, we enjoyed finger foods and lemonade. Laughter and camaraderie filled the uniquely decorated living room that evening. I enjoyed sweet dreams that night. It was worth taking time out of my schedule for my friend and me. I almost said no to her invitation; I practically was a no-show. God knew I needed a getaway. Putting aside troubles—if only for a couple of hours. That evening, I returned home and took up necessary responsibilities again. But in between, God allowed a much-needed escape. Reward: I returned with a much better attitude and outlook plus a bonus of a renewed friendship.

A friend is always loyal, and a brother is born to help in time of need—
Proverbs 17:17/NLT.

Day 56-60   Slip Away

- When was the last time you said yes to a fun event? Do you remember pausing to consult God first?
- Make a list of people who make you laugh and forget about yourself.
- After returning from the event, what emotions and feelings did you experience? Record how you felt after taking valuable time out for you. Re-visit these words when you have doubts about accepting a future event.

Day 58

Walk with the wise and become wise, for a companion of fools suffers harm— Proverbs 13:20.
*… associate with fools and get in trouble—*Proverbs 13:20/NLT.

Life is like a cup of coffee. Coffee is good, but a dollop of whipped cream on top makes it extra good! My dollops of whipped cream come when special friends ask me to join them for lunch or an evening out. Knowing we have a future time set aside to get together can make an insane-crazy week tolerable. Your time out could be accompanying a friend on an all day trip in a van loaded with young people for a school competition.

Be sure to pack a spirit of adventure and flexibility. Without planning, we become giddy and young again telling brand-new secrets. Cares and strained relationships back home soon fade away. Conversation flows from which brand of razor works best and fashion tidbits to advice on how to manage the men in our lives. One minute we laugh together, and the next share tears of sorrow. Let your hair down friends pick right up where they left off even if it's been six months or years since you last met. True-blue friendships are worthy investments. A quick phone call or note in the mail can bridge the gap. Other times, we plan walks through a local garden or along the beach.

After moving into a new home, decorating our sun porch was put on hold. I mentioned to my friend about the desire to create a retreat escape to read and write. She saw potential in my sun porch through objective, creative eyes and understood my vision. Vivid yellow, orange, hot pink and rose tones took shape as we focused on a focal point picture purchased earlier. Next, we went on a mission to a nearby fabric store. My seamstress-friend made a beeline for the right bolts of fabrics for pillows and curtains that would carry out my dream plan. Bless her heart—months later, I received a care package loaded with fun and funky handcrafted pillows and a prototype curtain.

Friends respect each other as unique individuals possessing value and worth. A sense of renewal and rejuvenation fills the soul. We're armed and ready to face the world—or at least active toddlers, or moody teenagers and a mountain of laundry. Reminds me of the Girl Scout campfire song,

> "Make new friends, but keep the old.
> One is silver, the other is gold.
> A circle is round; it has no end.
> That's how long, I will be your friend ...
> You help me, and I'll help you
> and together we will see it through"[30]

- Which friends do you feel are wise and have a positive influence on you? What is your battle plan to *walk with the wise*?
- Do you have a friend that falls into the fool category and causes you to get into trouble (mentioned in Proverbs 13)? What steps could you take in order to associate with the wise, those who help see you through the muck and mire?
- Think of a time when you associated with positive, wise people and how you felt afterward? What benefits lingered? Record your contemplations. This record can prove helpful in the future when in the midst of choosing a friend/activity.

Day 59

> "We can do no great things, only small things with great love,"
> Mother Teresa.

Date your husband regularly. Soon you will turn around and the children in your life grow up and move out. Then quickly, you too will join the empty nester club. I know because it happened to me. You think you have a long time to enjoy them and their myriad of activities. Truth is, life zooms past quicker than you would ever dream. I remember a particularly challenging day when I grumbled to my mom. *When would the diapers, laundry, grocery shopping, meal planning, house cleaning, and daily stuff ever end? How did I get myself into this slave mode?*

Even today, I hear my mom say, "Don't wish these days away. Before you know it, they'll be in school, dating, out of the house, and married with children of their own."

At the time, I thought, she did not know what she was talking about. It was as if someone hit the pause mode and I'd never see the light of day again. Guess what? She knew what she was talking about! I also homeschooled during this time. Even more reason to date my husband and take time for me. Time for me to grow spiritually in a Bible study setting and girlfriend time proved even more crucial.

Reminder: you married your spouse first; the children came second. Strive for a healthy balance between spouse/significant other, children, extended family, and work. The word overwhelming comes to mind. Quiet time with God, on the top of your to-do list, comes in handy. (Trust me, I know how DIFFICULT this is!) Use your spouse, trusted friend, or family member as an accountability partner and springboard for communication of your highs and lows. Evaluate and rate your progress periodically. Barter babysitting nights; I will take your children this week and you take mine the next date night. Going out to eat at a nice restaurant is wonderful, but also incorporate inexpensive dates such as a walk in the park or along a pier. The goal is to avoid turning around one day while gazing at our spouse and thinking, *Who are you, and where did you come from?* The best gift to your child: loving, quality time with your spouse.

Now I am an empty nester. *How did I get to this season already?* There are days I wish I could be magically granted a do-over. Days I was crabbier than I care to admit. Days I wish I cared less about cleanliness and more about being a loving, fun mom and wife. Relish every moment with each of your children individually and together as a family unit. There are no do-overs. One thing I am assured of is God's forgiveness. He forgave me; so I must forgive myself for messing up on occasion and move on. As I gaze at the present, I like to think He gave me a type of do-over as I strive to love, care, and pray for my dear grandchildren.

Day 56-60   *Slip Away*

Free—free at last
Free to roam, or
not to roam
I only have this moment in time
To do as I feel best
I pause

Swimmers swim
Sailors sail
Surfers surf
Athletes run
Babies cry
Lovers walk

This time feels surreal
Almost like guilty pleasure
I wait
For what, I cannot say
Oh yes, I know
To get nearer God to Thee

But the fruit of the Spirit is love, joy, peace, patience, kindness, goodness, faithfulness, gentleness, self-control. Against such there is no law—Galatians 5:22–23.

- Have you been a recipient of one of the fruits of the Spirit listed above? Describe the situation. Can you recall when you extended a fruit of the Spirit characteristic to someone? Record those memories.
- When did you last date your loved one with only him/her as your sole focus? What did you do and how did you feel afterwards? If you cannot remember the last time, it's time to plug a date into your calendar.
- Think about someone who could benefit from a gift of kindness or faithfulness. Next, pray and ask God's wisdom about a plan to extend the gift forward.

Day 60

As iron sharpens iron, so one person sharpens another—Proverbs 27:17.
... so a man sharpens the countenance of his friend—Proverbs 27:17/KJV.

Being around and involved with good people—people with like values and motives contributes to a healthy over-all existence. These friends keep me accountable to do and say what is honorable.

Last year, I was having a rough time celebrating a certain milestone birthday. A dear friend surprised me by showing up on my doorstep with a knowing smile on her face and a humorous book in her hand. I've been known to volunteer my husband's services (and my own) for high school graduation open houses and funeral gatherings. My husband and I surprised my friend by traveling nearly 500 miles on our motorcycle for her son's high school graduation. She had a permanent grin on her face the entire day because we chose to lend physical help and moral support.

Day 56-60   Slip Away

My mind goes to a friend who's an excellent model for me. She reminds me to take everything to God in prayer—like she does. We've shared a cup of tea/coffee, meals and perused small lakeshore town stores and thrift shops. When we get together, we care and share with one other. There is no need too great or too small that God doesn't want to hear about. We freely share our prayer requests, burdens, and answers to prayer. I know my go-to friend will pray for a need if she says she will.

As a mom, I pray for friends who would be a good influence on my children. Our children are not the only ones in need of good companions. Even as an adult, I benefit from rubbing shoulders with people who steer me in the right direction. Friends remind me of a past commitment, lovingly point out sin[31] in my life, or share a Bible verse at the right time. Speaking the truth in love. We need each other. Long term; we don't function well in isolation. God uses key characters in our lives to affirm, remind, and sometimes discipline us. It's for our own good.

- Think about someone in your life whom you could befriend. What would you do to initiate the friendship? Or, if you have someone in your life who influences you for the good, set a date with him/her strengthening that bond.
- Try to gain God's perspective on this friendship—what should this relationship look like in His eyes?
- Has someone spoken to you about a certain topic that pushed your hot button? How did you react to them? What truth may be lodged within their words?

Prayer of Encouragement:

Dear God, show me how to be a good friend. Not one that overlooks wrongs, but an honest and truthful friend. Help me be open and accountable to this person and vice versa. I want to know when to speak and when not to speak. Show me how a friendship works so that we will act in a way that pleases You. Amen.

Consider the ways God lovingly cares for you in Psalm 23 in several different translations.

Day 56-60   Slip Away

NOTES

Section 3

Soul (Life is Precious)

Day 61-65   Solitary Place

Chapter 13

Solitary Place

"When God gets us alone through suffering, heartbreak, temptation, disappointment, sickness, or by thwarted desires, a broken friendship, or a new friendship—when He gets us absolutely alone, and we are totally speechless, unable to even ask one question, then He begins to teach us ... or am I more concerned with my own ideas, friendships, and cares for my body? Jesus cannot teach me anything until I quiet all my intellectual questions and get alone with Him," Oswald Chambers.[32]

Oswald Chambers touches on nitty gritty life stuff. Have you ever been alone with God? Trials and temptations can send us back into the arms of God. *Why does it take a major trauma to seek Him? Knowing I can trust Him, why don't I go to Him first and skip the in-between stops?*

To be completely alone with zero distractions. Do you find yourself multi-tasking when on hold? Not wanting to waste time is my justification. Scrolling e-mails, answering text messages, perusing Facebook. While on hold during a conversation or riding an elevator, background music or random advertisements play. This constant vying for attention hinders deep thoughts and makes it difficult to hear His wisdom through all the interference.

In our small group, each of us chose one word to describe who we want to be and what we want to focus on during the next step of our journey. My one word: Listen. When I'm quiet and actually listening for His still, small voice,

Day 61-65   *Solitary Place*

I draw closer to Him. Miracles happen. Prayers get answered. Like young Samuel experienced in 1 Samuel 3:10–11,

The Lord came and stood there, calling as at the other times, "Samuel! Samuel!"
Then Samuel said, "Speak, for your servant is listening."
And the Lord said to Samuel: "See, I am about to do something in Israel that will make the ears of everyone who hears about it tingle."

How often do we go through the motions of checking off one task and immediately moving to the next? Usually there's not much of a break in-between to clear our heads from the last checklist. Where is God in this? Do we allow Him room to move and share His guidance in a busy, over-booked schedule?

Then if my people who are called by my name will humble themselves and pray and seek my face and turn from their wicked ways, I will hear from heaven and will forgive their sins and restore their land—2 Chronicles 7:14/NLT.

- Write out a definition for the following words using your choice of resources.

  Pride:

  _____

  Humility:

  _____

  Seek:

  _____

  Wisdom:

  _____

- Using the definitions you found, think about how those words are active in your life. Journal your thoughts.
- When was the last time you spent uninterrupted time in solitary prayer? Describe your environment during this time.
- What one word would you choose? Visit this website to help you decide: http://myoneword.org/word.

Prayer of Encouragement:

    Oh God, You are a loving God Who desires me to come to You. You want to hear about my joys and sorrows. Forgive me for not running to You first when I have a problem, a question, or when I need to soak up Your majesty and glory. I realize time with You will shape me into a suitable servant. Do away with my prideful spirit, stubbornness, and ignorance. Eagerly I anticipate valuable time spent alone with You, my God. Help me carve time out for You.

Day 61-65   Solitary Place

Day 61

My cup overflows—Psalm 23:5.

I continue to be amazed, surprised, and gladdened as more folks express their desire to come alongside and pray me through surgery. *God, I know that You are all I need, but it helps to have people available with skin and flesh on them too! Thank you, God. My patience runs thin. Weariness pervades my body. I know when I am weak, You are strong.*

Gazing around, I see God's gifts. I tend to reflect and realize my blessings when near water. The marina, where we dock our sailboat, stands virtually empty during the week. I feel carefree and lighthearted, but somewhat undecided in the midst of a sea of possibilities. Maybe, I'll do nothing at all. Thank God for this delightful freedom. Uplifting. Freeing to my body and brain. No distractions. I can think and write as the Holy Spirit directs my fingertips:

Sanctuary

Feeling of splendor

Of brightness—rightness

Calm. Serenity.

I can honestly say

It is well with my soul

No hurry—no worry

I can be—I can do

Without answering to anyone

Except my God

Life is: Good Fragile Precious

As I look across the water
Breakfast sandwich in hand
Sailboat cockpit reflects bright sun

Sanctuary. Alone time.
Which path shall I travel?
Your will be done, not mine

"There is nothing—absolutely nothing—half so much worth doing as simply messing about in boats," Kenneth Grahame, *The Wind in the Willows*.

- What do the words, *My cup overflows* mean to you? Record your thoughts.
- Name a few recent blessings from God's generous hands. Journal these gems for later review.
- Whom is your heart burdened for? Stop and pray asking God's hand of restoration and blessing in their life. If you choose, the acronym A.C.T.S. may help you follow a pattern for prayer. On the lines, write their names and your prayer.

      A. = Adoration: _____
      C. = Confession: _____
      T. = Thanksgiving: _____
      S. = Supplication: _____

Day 61-65   Solitary Place

Day 62

Very early in the morning, while it was still dark, Jesus got up, left the house and went off to a solitary place, where he prayed. Simon and his companions went to look for him, and when they found him, they exclaimed: Everyone is looking for you!—Mark 1:35–37.

Our lives probably do not involve raising people from the dead, casting out demons, or feeding the multitudes. We do manage challenging schedules while shuttling children back and forth from school, lessons, and sporting events. Some days it may feel like the four-wheel vehicle is your home. It's easy to think, *There is nowhere to go where I can really be alone. Someone always wants something from me. If only I had a few more hours in the day. If only my spouse would be more helpful or my children better behaved?*

While reading through the gospel of Mark, I catch a glimpse of Jesus' demanding daily schedule. Not only did Jesus mentor His chosen disciples, but throngs of people followed Him from town to town. *That evening after sunset the people brought to Jesus all the sick and demon-possessed. The whole town gathered at the door, and Jesus healed many who had various diseases* (Mark 1:32–34). The more miracles He performed, the more people flocked after Him making it nearly impossible for time alone with His Heavenly Father.

If Jesus felt it necessary to carve a piece of His day aside for meditation and prayer, how much **more** do I need this sacred time of renewal? C.S. Lewis wisely points out that no one was busier than Christ. "Our model is the Jesus … of the workshop, the roads, the crowds, the clamorous demands and surly oppositions, the lack of all peace and privacy, the interruptions … the Divine life operating under human conditions."

My insides are turned inside out; specters of death have me down. I shake with fear, I shudder from head to foot. Who will give me wings, I ask—wings like a dove? Get me out of here on dove wings; I want some peace and quiet. I want a walk in the country, I want a cabin in the woods. I'm desperate for a change from rage and stormy weather—Psalm 55:5–8/MSG.

- When is the best time to retreat to a secluded place and lay your burdens down to the God of all comfort and healing? Understand this is not a one-time event. Plan mini and maxi-retreats. Daily, weekly, monthly, quarterly, or one or two times a year if possible.
- Where do you go to be isolated and silent before God? Jot down several concrete ideas. If you haven't gone there for a while, what hinders you from going? Some may need a scheduled respite once a day; others once a week to keep chaos at bay.
- Name the last time you felt compassion to pray on behalf of others? Explain.

Day 63

So let us come boldly to the throne of our gracious God. There we will receive his mercy, and we will find grace to help us when we need it most—Hebrews 4:16/NLT.

In our church community, there is a group of dedicated, talented women who faithfully hand knit prayer shawls. As the saintly ladies create the lovely shawls, each stitch is bathed in prayer. Prayer for the person's physical and emotional needs, for the family and friends who will be their caretakers before, during, and after surgery. They pray for people in desperate need of healing; people the crafters may not have ever met.

The prayer shawl, or tallit gadol[33] in Hebrew, is an object full of symbolism. Wrapping oneself in the shawl signifies being surrounded by the encompassing light of the Creator. Each part of the garment contains features that remind the wearer of powerful ideas in Judaism.

I have witnessed the presentation of a special prayer shawl for others undergoing serious health issues. This was a first for me when my group of Bible study ladies wrapped a beautiful red shawl around my shoulders and prayed for me personally. Tears flowed freely; tears of joy and love. The awesome privilege of being included in someone else's prayers left me speechless. I felt blessed to the brim to be a part of this amazing love ministry.

Daily I receive encouraging calls, notes, and emails assuring me of prayers. I am grateful for God's love showered upon us in tangible and intangible ways. I stand amazed in His presence!

> "Our enemies will pursue us deliberately into our very prayer rooms. The only way in which we can gather and keep collected our distracted minds and roaming thoughts is to center them about Jesus Christ."[34]

- Is there someone who could use a visit from you, or a prayer said on their behalf? Write out their name and your plan of action.
- Are there areas you choose to go your own way? In what areas do you follow God and His desires for your life? Be specific.
- Go boldly and ask God for His infinite mercy and grace in a specific area of your life. Formulate the prayer in writing. Often I find it helpful to thumb through the pages of a hymnal and sing or speak back priceless words from a song. A newer tune, *Your Grace Still Amazes Me,* by Phillips, Craig & Dean, speaks of the mystery of God's grace. Does God's grace still amaze you?

Your grace still amazes me
Your love is still a mystery
Each day I fall on my knees
'cause your grace still amazes me
Your grace still amazes me!

Day 64

And the Holy Spirit helps us in our weakness. For example, we don't know what God wants us to pray for. But the Holy Spirit prays for us with groanings that cannot be expressed in words—Romans 8:26/NLT.

Waiting and writing contain similar characteristics. Both activities often done in solo. Waiting: such as waiting for a doctor's appointment or surgery date is mainly done alone. Right now, I am waiting at a lab for a comprehensive blood test. Often, I don't know how to pray for a particular resolution or answer to my quandary. I find it fascinating when I fumble for the right words (which is often); the Holy Spirit fills in the gap and prays for me. Divine comfort fills my spirit.

Family members and friends pray and think of me during this time. However, I'm the one alone on that rolling table that will pass through sterile silver doors. There is One who accompanies me. My God. The One who never leaves or forsakes me—no matter what—no matter how I feel, act, or re-act. He is always there for me. Can it get any better than this? I'm not sure how. Do I have problems and unanswered questions? Yes, but I am still truly blessed and choose to praise Him. "Learning to take care of ourselves is worthwhile and nurturing. Jesus did it; so can we."[35]

Day 61-65   Solitary Place

But Jesus often withdrew to lonely places and prayed—Luke 5:16.

- When did you last spend soulful, quiet time listening (there's that word listen again) to God? What did you hear from God?
- Do you feel the enemy trying to block you from doing what you know is right? If so, in what ways? In what circumstances does this occur?
- What specific event or answer to prayer are you waiting for? Journal those areas in which you wait expectantly.

Day 65

She had a sister called Mary, who sat at the Lord's feet listening to what he said. But Martha was distracted by all the preparations that had to be made. She came to him and asked, Lord, don't you care that my sister has left me to do the work by myself? Tell her to help me! Martha, Martha, the Lord answered, you are worried and upset about many things, but only one thing is needed. Mary has chosen what is better, and it will not be taken away from her— Luke 10:39.

"When I get up in the morning, I sit on the side of my bed and say, God, if I don't get anything else done today, I want to know You more and love You better. God didn't put me on earth just to fulfill a to-do list. He's more interested in what I am than what I do. That's why we're called human beings, not human doings."[36]

Jesus and His disciples visited the village home of His friends, Mary and Martha. Relaxed and comfortable, Mary sits at her Lord's feet. Nearby, her sister Martha frets and runs around preparing food for the guests. What Martha is doing needs to be done and it's all good stuff, but possibly the timing and her attitude needs a slight adjustment.

When I hear this story, I ask myself, *so which one do I emulate, Mary or Martha?* Sad to say, I more likely resemble Martha. I do not consider myself to have OCD (Obsessive-Compulsive Disorder), but I prefer to plan ahead of time rather than tackling tasks at the last minute or leaving them undone.

Martha seems more caught up in details, making everything perfect so others will think highly of her and her preparations. Jesus states that *Mary has chosen what is better.* She chose to sit, listen, and worship. *Be still and know that I am God* (Psalm 46:10). *The Lord of Heaven's Armies is here among us!* (Psalm 46:7/NLT). Concentration on important business. There is a time to pause and listen to Jesus and a time to work for Him. I want to hear God say to me, "Teresa, you have chosen what is better."

While anticipating future events, focus on God. Not on what can be received from God or people, but how to grow spiritually. Keeping in step, not going ahead or lagging behind the Heavenly Father. Friends and family desire time with me on the days leading up to surgery. I'm thankful for that, yet part of me pulls away wanting to guard this precious interval. Is this selfishness, or self-preservation and loving myself properly? I like to think of it as loving myself.

> "To sit still … for me, that's the posture of Mary—the still prayer of waiting that transforms us in unseen ways," Sue Monk Kidd.

Day 61-65   Solitary Place

- Mary or Martha: whom do you more closely resemble and in what ways?
- On a scale of 1-10 (ten being the highest), how tired and emotionally stressed are you right now? What factor contributes to the number you chose?
- In what situation do you find it hard to wait on God and His timing? Be specific.

Prayer of Encouragement:

Dear God, thank you for this time You provided so I could lie down in green pastures and beside quiet waters. You know me inside out and upside down. There are no secrets from You. You alone know how much I truly savor quiet. You're in the continual process of soul restoration guiding me in paths of righteousness … beside me comforting me. For this reason, I need not fear any evil—Your mercy, goodness, and love are with me. My cup overflows as I look forward to dwelling in Your house forever. Love, from a daughter of the King.

Read through Psalm 46 in several different translations. Ponder, meditate, and highlight key phrases that touch your spirit and soul.

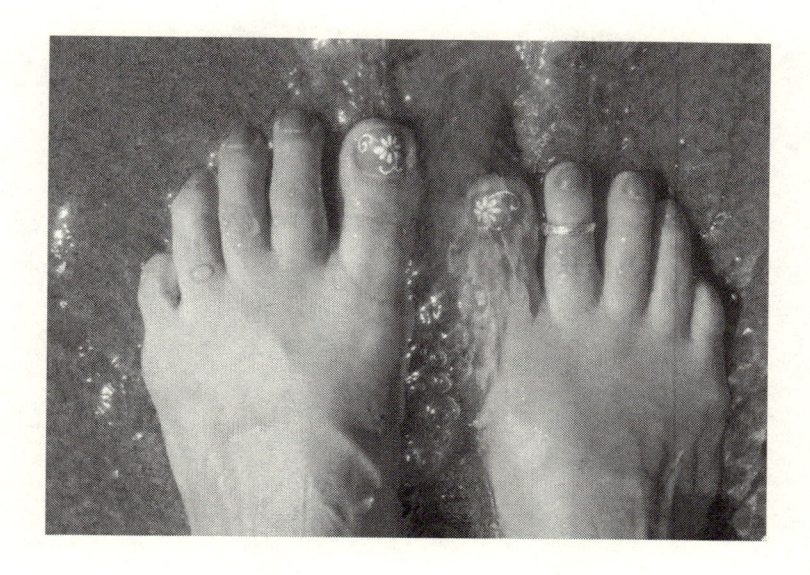

Chapter 14

All Other Ground is Sinking Sand

But everyone who hears these sayings of Mine, and does not do them, will be like a foolish man who built his house on the sand: and the rain descended, the floods came, and the winds blew and beat on that house; and it fell. And great was its fall—
Matthew 7:26-27/NKJV.

I need to come to this oasis for a temporary escape from chaos and everyday life cares. I drove to the Lake Michigan shoreline and allowed the water and sound of water to calm my mind and soul. In this quiet place, it seemed natural and easy to worship my Creator.

Seagulls chattered and plunged in the waves. A distant mourning dove sang his song of lament. As I walked along the cool water's edge, sand oozed between my toes. Water rippled evenly, consistently. A light breeze stirred in

Day 66-70   All Other Ground is Sinking Sand

the air and played with my hair as if to say, *Hello, I am still here—remember me?* Ah, yes, how can I forget You, God ... You have been there for me through past blessings and trials.

God was near then and is near now. He waits for me to communicate, pray, and meditate on Scripture. God knows the beginning and the end, and will see me through surgery and beyond. Regardless of the outcome, God cares and has my best interests in mind. My responsibility is to place myself in the healthiest position possible to prepare for surgery and subsequent recovery. This means time alone with God allowing Him to love and care for me. The key to launching a firm foundation lies in your belief system. Can you confirm or validate those beliefs?

> "She kept swimming out into life because she hadn't yet found a rock to stand on," Barbara Kingsolver.

- Is there something or someone in your life you are leaning more heavily on than Christ, the Solid Rock? Create a list of those things or people. Have you found a rock to stand on? If you have, describe that rock. Who/what do you believe in or trust?
- Describe a heavy rain or stormy situation that rocked your world (or may be rocking it right now). How do you plan to withstand the next storm of life?
- Check your foundation. What type of foundation are you building on? Solid, firm, or wobbly and inferior?

Everyone who hears these words of mine and puts them into practice is like a wise man who built his house on the rock. The rain came down, the streams rose, and the winds blew and beat against that house; yet it did not fall, because it had its foundation on the rock— Matthew 7:24–25.

Prayer of Encouragement:

Dear Father, I want to be like the wise person who builds their house upon a rock solid foundation. My desire is to listen to Your words and put them into practice. I pray that I fix my eyes on nothing or no one else but You, my Solid Rock.

Day 66

Fearing people is a dangerous trap, but trusting the Lord means safety— Proverbs 29:25/NLT.

Oh the joy of hearing raindrops pitter-patter over my head and against the window. Never mind that it is before 5:00 in the morning, my medication's worn thin, and the ice pack on my throbbing head melted. I am alive! Rain unfettered by overhead hospital beams and medical personnel busily performing clinical duties. Normal people carry on routine activities. Hallelujah, my surgery is over and the doctors feel it was successful. It's good; it's all good. This truly is a day to rejoice and be glad in it! I feel refreshed by God. He restores my soul.

Now folks, there's a slight gap here. A few details I remember, other pieces I found out later. Some aspects my daughter recorded for me. This I do know: Steve took the part of our marriage vows about being faithful in sickness

Day 66-70   All Other Ground is Sinking Sand

and in health seriously. He took time off work and slept on an uncomfortable hospital chair. When I could not feed myself, he fed me spoonfuls of oatmeal. After the neurosurgeon and plastic surgeon specialist finished their work, many staples closed my scalp and facial area back together. Steve patiently scrubbed my bloody, stapled scalp day after day until the staple removal day.

Our daughter, Amanda, also took time off work to care for me and proved a source of great support. My son, Andrew, and family from Minnesota volunteered to come if I needed them. Feeling the love as family members and friends across the United States prayed for and encouraged us.

> "I'll love you, dear, I'll love you
> Till China and Africa meet,
> And the river jumps over the mountain
> And the salmon sing in the street"[37]

- When was the last time you feared what other people thought about you (your looks, clothing, vehicle you drive, or house you live in)? Journal those fears.
- Recall a time someone did something nice for you that was totally unexpected. How did you feel? How difficult was it to accept the kindness? (Or, maybe it wasn't hard at all)
- Describe a situation when you felt God's hand of protection over you or your family? Take time now to thank Him for that divine protection.

Day 67

God gives us "just enough light for the step I'm on."[38]

My job is to reach out in the darkness and find His hand. I'd love to know the end result. *After the brain surgery, will there be any lasting effects? Will I suffer seizures? If I do, will I be able to drive again? What about regaining my balance and original facial features?* Curiously, God does not give us more information than needed. He illuminates the step just in front of us, but probably not many more. Why? I'm guessing He doesn't feel we can handle an abundance of information. He gives us just enough data to carry out our duties and then asks that we wait on Him for further details. Dependence on Him. Each and every day is a precious gift from God.

I took my first walk outdoors with supervision and the aid of a walker. Walking on the sidewalk to the end of our driveway plus another round, I felt a freedom rush! Fresh air. A type of release from bondage in the bed.

What a difference sleeping through the whole night without medical staff interruptions and noisy non-stop hospital sounds. Steve fixed my first post-surgery bacon and cheese omelet with brown sugar muffins for breakfast. I was able to leisurely sleep in and savor a hot cup of cherry tea from my neighbor. Friends and family bring yummy, home-made meals, give hugs, and send cards, prayers, well wishes, flowers and plants.

When Jesus spoke again to the people, he said, I am the light of the world. Whoever follows me will never walk in darkness, but will have the light of life—John 8:12.

- Are you feeling in the dark regarding some aspect of your life? If so, describe in what way.
- Do you know your life's purpose? Record those thoughts in your journal.
- Recall and describe the last situation where you intentionally followed *the light of the world,* Jesus–God, and it seemed really odd or impractical to do what He said.

Day 68

For everything that was written in the past was written to teach us, so that through the endurance taught in the Scriptures and the encouragement they provide, we might have hope … May the God of hope fill you (Teresa—fill in your name) *with all joy and peace as you* (Teresa) *trust in Him, so that you* (Teresa) *may overflow with hope by the power of the Holy Spirit*—Romans 15:4, 13.

Hope is a huge word. As believers, we hope in the one, true God. Rich, my former boss, reminded me of the above verse and suggested I fill in my name where appropriate. He consoled me with the fact that things take care of themselves and will be just fine. If I don't do them; someone else will handle the tasks. My job now is to do what I need to do in order to regain my health and strength. To be in the position God would have me in at this point in my life. All this sage advice coming from a person who endured numerous brain surgeries himself! I see God showing up just when I needed encouragement. He sent Rich who shared with me from his heart and life experiences. Rich touched a place in my soul. No one else could have reached me in quite the same way unless they had walked this perilous unknown road.

Did I miss a week of life? Partly that's okay—the part that hurt, the painful, sordid details part anyway. Sometimes in the morning, Steve and I chat. He fills me in on some of the missing pieces of those weeks gone by when I ask questions. Like when did I have trouble breathing after surgery? Foggy, patchy memories come back from time to time. I vaguely remember our daughter, Amanda, begging me to breathe.

"Mom, breathe, breathe!" She repeated that plea time after time until finally I did breathe. I vaguely recall choking and sputtering. Apparently 20 or so medical personnel descended on me trying to get me to breathe. Eventually I responded to Amanda's voice only and breathed. Life was good again. In some respects, it feels as if only a day or two has passed. Other times, it feels much longer. Like someone else's body and not mine. I am blessed and thankful God gave me a brand-new lease on life. An involved coach watches over me—not a distant bystander. While reading in Psalm 33:18–22, I discover more of what God does for His children:

- His eye is on me as I hope in His unfailing love. Who else does that all the time? No one.
- He is my helper and shield. Knowledge of this brings great solace.
- Rejoicing comes as I trust in His holy name.
- Yes, it is okay to be a joy-filled believer; in fact, joyfulness is encouraged.

My hope is in God. Anywhere else would be misplaced trust. Unfailing love—all the time.

- Name a time when you desperately needed hope. What means did you use for coping?
- Did you find that hope? If so, where or from whom?
- Record some verses to cling to that give you hope. Accumulate a running list for these go-to verses.

Day 69

Fear of man will prove to be a snare, but whoever trusts in the Lord is kept safe— Proverbs 29:25.

There are many voices for us to listen to in this day and age. Sometimes people's words ring out louder than God's message to us. Are those voices actually louder? Maybe our ears are not tuned to the proper channel. Listening to or following people can prove to be a trap. We can become entangled with other practices or doctrines without giving a second thought to our true, internal beliefs.

Our former Pastor Ed would often add a disclaimer to his words, "Don't take my word for it, go to the Bible and search out the answers for yourself. See what God has to say about the subject." I appreciate his humbleness and importance of placing glory and credit where they belong. God's Word should always supersede any words spoken or written by man. The Bible suggests seeking wise counsel, but the ultimate source should be God.

I experienced a good night's sleep the night before, but last night was not so good. Medication helps to ward off the majority of headaches and pain. My visiting nurse encouraged me to not try to be a hero and withstand the pain. She says continue to medicate when needed so my body can attend to its healing process. I am well taken care of with the generosity from my husband, family, and friends bestowing gifts of food, cards, e-mail messages, and phone calls. Love and blessings surround us.

Restless nights. I'm awake every few hours alternating between one painkiller and another attempting to relieve the pain. My scalp itches due to the 30+ stitches. Soon the staples will come out and that will equal a glorious day. My thoughts are scattered making my notes scattered too. Waiting to see the physical therapist, but in the meantime I continue to do the arm and leg exercises learned in the hospital. Thank you, Lord, for placing the sun in my window over my chair.

"Living in dependence on me is the way to abundant life … When you are with other people, you often lose sight of My Presence. Your fear of displeasing people puts you in bondage to them, and they become your primary focus," Sue Monk Kidd.

- Where do you spend most of your time and money? What does this say about who you are trying to please and what you seek?
- Has this person or thing been a positive or negative influence in your life? (See question above). List a few concrete examples.
- What messages from God's Word do you need to apply to your personal life regarding friendships? Begin compiling an ongoing reference list. Here are a few references to get you started: Ecclesiastes 4:9–12; Proverbs 4:17–27; 12:26; 18:24.

Day 66-70   *All Other Ground is Sinking Sand*

Day 70

The thief comes only to steal and kill and destroy; I have come that they may have life, and have it to the full—John 10:10.

The enemy wants nothing more than to destroy our happiness. He may go after a loved one, spouse, or family member. Satan knows exactly where our weakness lies. He goes for the jugular in a subtle way. So subtle that you may not know you are the target. And then the arrow flies; the attack occurs before you know what hit you.

God's message is entirely opposite. He harbors no hidden agenda. Jesus came in the form of a human baby, grew into a man, suffered, and died on the cross. He rose again the third day so that we might have life. God delights when we manifest joy. His desire is that our joy be full. Living life to the fullest gives Him great pleasure.

I thought I'd go through the ceiling when the surgeon's assistant removed the first few staples along my forehead. Then she went a different track along my ear and those pulled out easier. Both the surgeon and his assistant gave us the good news that healing is progressing better than anticipated. They said I am looking good. I think they were just being kind to me. No more staples—Hallelujah, I'm a very happy girl!

As far as my exercise routine, here's my progress:

- I can stand on my own
- Ability to move my hands and arms unassisted
- See to make my way to the snack bar, bend and stretch
- Hear and obey instructions from physical and occupational therapists
- Schedule an appointment for the next therapist visit

I may be tired, slow and deliberate, but I'm alive, well and thankful. Life is good, fragile and precious. I dare not take life and living for granted. As far as facial scars, we have no clue how that will ultimately turn out. Pride looked at my face upon rising and I barely recognized the left side. Right side remains fairly consistent. *Who is the person behind those bloodshot puffy eyes? Where did those hues of purple and red come from?* One friend remarked that it must have been quite a fight. My response, "If you think I look bad, you should see the other guy!"

My jaw bone is in a state of healing after disturbing the nerve and my cheeks look swollen. It is a miracle I'm alive and healing so quickly. My sole responsibility is to take care of myself the best way I know how by doing my therapy regularly and eating properly. Once I take care of the small items, I will be entrusted with larger goals. I must take a break now; my head's churning and my eyes need rest.

I close my eye lids and these words to a hymn come to mind, *Only trust Him, only Trust Him now. He will save you, He will save you, and He will save you now … He will surely give you rest by trusting in His word* [39]

> "Wherever Jesus may lead us, He goes before us; if we don't know where we're going, we know with whom we go," Charles Spurgeon.

Day 66-70 All Other Ground is Sinking Sand

- Name a few of your weak spots. You don't have to show your list to anyone if you choose not to.
- Recall (if you dare) a time when you felt the presence of darkness and the enemy at work in your life. Record in your journal.
- Is your life satisfying? If not, what do you feel would make it more satisfying? Compile a go-to list of songs/hymns that focus your attention on the Savior and King.

Prayer of Encouragement:

I must give you the reins, God. You, and only you, know the beginning and the end of my journey. I trust you fully. Selfish desires be gone; you are in control! Help me keep my priorities in the right order. My desire is for you to be my top priority and the basis for my firm foundation. Forgive me for not always acting as though you are my boss. Now may the Lord of peace Himself give me peace at all times and in everything. Amen.

Re-read the account of the torrential floods in Matthew 7:21–29 in several different translations. What new insights did you uncover?

Chapter 15

Faith and Nature Unite

"To plant a garden is to believe in tomorrow," Audrey Hepburn.

"The discovery of a new dish does more for the happiness of mankind than the discovery of a star," Brillat-Savarin.

    I was born in the town of Ottumwa,[40] Iowa in Wapello County. Just a bit of trivia: Ottumwa is also the home of Cpl. Walter Eugene "Radar" O'Reilly—fictional corporal and company clerk from the book, movie, and popular television series *M*A*S*H*. Ottumwa is mentioned as Radar's hometown in the novel and regularly on the show. My family and I moved away from Iowa when I was very young and lived in several different states and cities.

    My husband and I live in a modest condominium, along with the rules and regulations associated with condo living. Huge, vast gardens are not on the horizon for this lady without a green thumb. However, while cooped up for

Day 71-75   *Faith and Nature Unite*

the long, winter months in Michigan, my mind began to dream of succulent fresh, leafy greens, home grown and ready to pick. My girlfriend tills a spacious garden in her backyard. She assured me a deck planter could work, and was willing to teach me.

I had the tools needed to realize my dream of home-grown vegetables. Keeping a deck planter high above the ground meant no worries about rabbits or other critters carrying away my treasures. Better yet, there was little room for weeds. I would have the convenience of walking a short distance to my deck, and viola´, fresh produce ripe for the picking. Side note: my name Teresa comes from Greek origin, meaning to harvest.

Light green lettuce dances in my deck planter mingled with basil, cilantro, oregano, hot banana pepper and a green pepper. When the tiny lettuce seeds popped their heads up through the black soil, I was amazed. Tender shoots appeared without first withering and dying. Normally, the only plants that survive at my house were cacti due to sheer neglect of watering and care.

My reaction reminded me of the parable Jesus told about a tiny mustard seed, *Because you have so little faith. I tell you the truth, if you have faith as small as a mustard seed, you can say to this mountain, move from here to there and it will move. Nothing will be impossible for you* (Matthew 17:20). The bounty enjoyed reminds me that God rewards even the tiniest seed of faith.

Then Christ will make his home in your hearts as you trust in him. Your roots will grow down into God's love and keep you strong—Ephesians 3:17/NLT.

- Is your faith strong and evident enough so that a neighbor can detect it? Are your roots growing deep and strong? If so, in what way?
- What or whom stands in your way of moving a mountain? Is there a step of faith you have not been able to take due to fear? Record that roadblock and your next step of faith to counteract the roadblock.
- Think of an answer to prayer you could share with a neighbor, friend, or family member. Then ask God for an opportunity to share that answer.

Prayer of Encouragement:

You are a great and awesome God, worthy to be praised and adored. As I look around me, there are many wonders to behold. Too many to count. You have gifted me these miracles to see, taste, and enjoy. Given freely without reserve. Let me never take them for granted. I want to be ready to share Your goodness and mercies every day. Thank you for Your gifts of kindness and sustenance.

Day 71

Then Job answered the Lord and said: I know that You can do everything, and that no purpose of Yours can be withheld from You—Job 42:1, 2/NKJV.

Throughout the book of Job, the age old question of *why* continues to pop up. Job was a righteous, prosperous farmer living in the land of Uz. He suffered much; losing valuable livestock, possessions, children, and eventually his own health. Yet, he still chose to praise God—regardless. *Naked I came from my mother's womb, and naked I will depart. The Lord gave and the Lord has taken away; may the name of the Lord be praised* (Job 1:21). Job realized that God is in charge of everything including nature, unexplained pain, and suffering. God is great and way *beyond our understanding* (Job 36:26). Our duty is to remain faithful to the God who created the entire universe. Nothing is impossible with God.

One morning, I lounged on the sofa with little ambition. Tired of waiting, researching, and answering people's questions, I listened to the radio. The station played these words ... loves like a hurricane ... bending beneath the weight of His wind and mercy ... and O how He loves me![41] On Sunday at church, the choir and orchestra sang the same song. I detect a repetition here; God reinforcing His love to me. I love how He speaks—particularly when I take the time to listen.

> *Though the fig tree does not bud*
> *and there are no grapes on the vines,*
> *though the olive crop fails*
> *and the fields produce no food,*
> *though there are no sheep in the pen*
> *and no cattle in the stalls,*
> *yet I will rejoice in the Lord,*
> *I will be joyful in God my Savior.*
> *The Sovereign Lord is my strength;*
> *he makes my feet like the feet of a deer,*
> *he enables me to tread on the heights.*
>
> (Habakkuk 3:17-19)

- Record an example when you felt God's power evident in your life?
- What are you willing to trust God with ... your health outcome? Family? Finances? Your love life? All of the above; none of the above? This is your choice.
- In what way do you feel God's affection and mercy toward you right now? Be specific.

Day 72

Consider it pure joy, my brothers, whenever you face trials of many kinds, because you know that the testing of your faith develops perseverance—James 1:2–3.

Growing a garden is not for the faint of heart. Consistent watering, knowing correct soil combinations, pruning, and fertilizing are key ingredients for success. I once took a leaf sample to my local garden center for advice about pests. He suggested a remedy that eventually saved my plant.

In our personal lives, we encounter troubles. We are not equipped to handle it all alone. Other people can point us in the right direction; however, God should be our first go-to source of wisdom. I will be the first to admit that I do not always seek God's wisdom first. Keeping the communication lines open takes work and effort. He created us and knows every fiber of our being. We might not receive what we ask for because it is not in our best interest. He longs for me to ask and be in constant communion with Him. Waiting develops character and perseverance. Pray for wisdom regarding the next step.

"When life throws you lemons, you make lemonade," James Brady.

Day 71-75   Faith and Nature Unite

- When was the last time you encountered a hurdle and considered it joy? Write down the moment you felt the joy.
- How did you journey through the struggle? What advice would you give a fellow pilgrim?
- In what way is your faith being tested now? Give an example. Record your thoughts and review your insights a week later; a month later.

Day 73

Another translation tells us more of Job's story, Job stood up and tore his robe in grief. Then he shaved his head and fell to the ground to worship. He said, I came naked from my mother's womb, and I will be naked when I leave. The Lord gave me what I had, and the Lord has taken it away. Praise the name of the Lord! In all of this, Job did not sin by blaming God— Job 1:20–22/NLT.

Job realized that God is in charge of nature and of unexplained pain and suffering. Even though he endured many trials, Scripture says Job did not sin. He did not blame God through it all. What an amazing attitude and perspective Job possessed! An attitude and outlook we would do well to imitate. I am pretty sure I would be looking for someone or something to blame all those calamities on.

"When God finally spoke, He didn't offer Job an answer [for his trials and tribulations]. Instead, He drove home the point that it is better to know God than to know answers."[42] Our duty is to remain faithful to the God who created the entire universe. Nothing is impossible with God. If He wills it, the event will take place. I can speculate day after day until eternity, but I will never fully understand God. *For my thoughts are not your thoughts, neither are your ways my ways* (Isaiah 55:8/NIV).

"A preacher of the gospel cannot meet the demands made upon him alone, any more than the vine can bear grapes without branches. The men who sit in the pews are to be the fruit-bearing ones. They are to translate the "ideal" of the pulpit into the "real" of daily life and action. But they will not do it they cannot do it, if they be not devoted to God and much given to prayer. Devotion to God and devotion to prayer are one and the same thing," E. M. Bounds.[43]

- How much time are you willing to invest in prayer and getting to know the God of the Universe in a more intimate way? What is your reasoning for that amount of time?
- Do you know anyone that possesses Job's godly perspective of praising God no matter what? What take-away advice do you see from them or Job's actions and words?
- What are some unanswered why issues in your mind? Record these in your journal and formulate a conversational prayer back to God.

Day 74

Where were you when I laid the earth's foundation? Tell me, if you understand—Job 38:4.

When the Roman soldiers sought to arrest Jesus in an olive grove, he knew what they wanted and who they were after.

"Who is it you want?"

"Jesus of Nazareth," they replied.

"I am," Jesus said.

Immediately, the whole host of soldiers, chief priests and Pharisees *drew back and fell to the ground.* (John 18:6) They could not help themselves. The great God had spoken. He is the Alpha and Omega, beginning and the end.

A small stuffed green frog reminds me to rely on this same great God. Pastor Ray, our church visiting pastor, presented me with a stuffed, green frog in the hospital after surgery. He explained to me that Froggie was no ordinary frog; F.R.O.G. stands for **Fully Rely On God**.

After leaving the hospital, Froggie now travels with me in airplanes, cars, and boats. You might find him next to a sand bucket on the beach, a playground, or attending church services, etc. When not in travel mode, he perches next to my computer as a constant reminder to consider God in all I do and say. I repeat those poignant words: **Fully Rely On God**. That phrase brings my mind, body, and soul back to where I need to focus. Froggie reminds me of Who is really in charge of life in sickness, health, prosperity, or hard times. Regardless.

"Feed your faith and your fears will starve to death."[44]

Life is: Good Fragile Precious

- Do you question some aspect of your life, such as: sickness, infertility, depression, unemployment, or the inability to find a life soul mate? Name those hot button topics.
- Referring to the question above, was God fair or kind when He allowed this to happen (or not happen)? How are you dealing with the situation? Explain your perspective.
- Are you willing to accept God's ways as part of His overall plan? What part of that plan do you accept: all or just part of His ways/solution? How can you wrap yourself around the F.R.O.G. concept and how might that change your life?

Day 75

Who has a claim against me that I must pay? Everything under heaven belongs to me— Job 41:11.

Gardening is such a wonderful, fun teaching time with children and grandchildren. My granddaughter, Liberty, loves watering my deck planters when she visits. Every day, we checked the growth progress of the tomatoes, green pepper, and lettuce. I remember her zeal when she picked that first green pepper. My grandchildren eagerly lead me to the deck to inspect the status of our vegetables and herbs.

"Is it time to water the plants yet, Nana?" they diligently ask.

"Good idea; I think it's time to check on them!"

When I look at my homegrown garden, I think about the original Garden of Eden. I marvel at God's creation ... the heavens and earth, light and darkness, sky and water, land and vegetation, fish and birds, man and woman. He gives us boundless provisions every day, if I choose to look intently all around me.

Gardeners enjoy the hunt for just the right plant or flower for their garden, porch, or patio. Later comes the eating of home-grown delicious and nutritious fresh garden herbs and salad greens. Who doesn't marvel at the matchless beauty of a flower or a tender shoot of lettuce? (See recipe for Tortellini Salad and other favorites in the back of the book).

"You don't stop gardening when you get old; you grow old when you stop gardening," Unknown.

- In what location might you design a flower or vegetable garden? How might this garden be healthy for you and your loved ones?
- When was the last time you enjoyed God's creation? Plan a walk outdoors in a park, garden, zoo, or in your own neighborhood. Record your observations including how the walk affected you.
- What things or people has God planted in your life to point you back to Him and His amazing creation?

Prayer of Encouragement:

    Dear God, I realize what happens in my life is already pre-orchestrated by You. I truly want to be content. My desire is to tell You thank you more often and use less why and why not words. Help me use my ears and pause to listen. I have much to be thankful for: my healing body, family, home, food on the table, freedom of speech and freedom of worship. You are a great and awesome God!

Read through Chapter 38 of Job listing miracles God accomplished.

Day 71-75   Faith and Nature Unite

Granddaughter Liberty

Chapter 16

Little Eyes Watch

For physical training is of some value, but godliness has value for all things, holding promise for both the present life and the life to come ... Don't let anyone look down on you because you are young, but set an example for the believers in speech, in life (conduct), in love, in faith and in purity—1 Timothy 4:8, 12.

"Me and my Mumma's going to church now," declares Liberty, my 3½ year old granddaughter. Off she marches with her Bible under her left arm, and baby doll (named Mumma) in her right hand. It wasn't long before I heard her chattering in another part of our house. Upon further investigation, I found her settled on the sofa telling a Bible story to her dolly and reciting lines from her church Christmas program. The morning before, Liberty cuddled next to me while I read my devotions content to be near Nana.

Studying God's Word, reading Bible stories, and speaking kindly—our actions really do matter. In her young mind, the habit of attending church with Dad and Mom became customary. Children watch and model adult behavior in their small sphere of influence.

Oh, be careful little eyes what you see. For the Father up above is looking down in love, my own children learned this song at a young age. The song warns little ears to be careful what you hear, tongue what you say, hands what you do, feet where you go, mind what you think, and heart whom you trust. Nothing is missed with their young, keen radar. Big people would do well heeding these warnings also.

Liberty and her younger siblings represent my best reasons for keeping a scheduled quiet time with my heavenly Father. I truly want to be a strong, stable influence. When I read through the virtues and guide for modeling godly behavior in Proverbs 31, a dear friend named Nancy comes to mind. Mentor and surrogate mom after my mom passed, she represented one of only two people (other than family) whom mom allowed to visit during her last days in the hospital. I also had the privilege of her tutelage in Bible study groups. Weekly she would share wise words from Scripture along with everyday practical life applications. One particular saying of hers remains a favorite of mine, Bitter or Better? When seemingly bad things happen, will you allow this event to cause you to grow bitter, or will it make you better?

In third grade, my mom taught Nancy's son, Jim, in Sunday school class. She tells the story that he came home one day excited that he had a new Sunday school teacher,

"And guess what? She has the same name as me!"

It's true, my mom's name was Jimmie and that's what they called her son. Years later, a large group of believers refer to Jim as Pastor Jim, our senior pastor. Words and actions count. When we choose to trust and obey, we never know what ripple effects may result.

> "It is the wise mother who gives her child roots and wings,"
> Chinese Proverb.

- What precautions do you take for being careful about what your eyes feast on, your hands do, and where your feet take you? List some precautions in your journal.
- Take a step back, list a few sarcastic or critical words you remember voicing recently. Record your most recent thankful and uplifting words. (Bravo to you!)
- What examples are you setting for the people in your sphere of influence? How do you offer those young people roots and wings?

Prayer of Encouragement:

Father, I desperately want to be a good example and role model for others, especially to my impressionable grandchildren. Grant me grace so that my walk matches my talk. May I lead a godly life of faith, love, and purity all the days You choose for me to live on earth. I trust in Your supernatural strength and wisdom. Amen.

Day 76-80   Little Eyes Watch

Day 76

Charm is deceptive, and beauty is fleeting; but a woman who fears the Lord is to be praised— Proverbs 31:30.

The virtuous woman, or a wife of noble character, is described as being clothed with strength and dignity. She speaks with wisdom, and faithful instruction is on her tongue. Sometimes I jokingly say, "God gave me a second chance to get this parenting job correct. He gave me grandchildren."

We can dress nice and look pretty without being entirely occupied on how we look to outsiders. Focus should not be on capturing someone's attention or making sure I am wearing the latest trendy style. Praise comes from the Lord when I give Him the proper respect and time He so richly deserves. Seeking people's approval accomplishes no good thing. I have far to go along the path of becoming this virtuous model. Life is a journey and I know I am on the right path. Modeling godly behavior takes time and energy, but the rewards equal tremendous joy that money cannot buy. Godly conduct reaps benefits that might not be seen in this lifetime. Results may show up in the second, third, and fourth generations. When I'm long gone.

My grandchildren love spending time in the kitchen. Liberty's child-size apron is bright red with plaid trim embroidered with the words, Cookie Taster. Tucked away in a kitchen drawer for when they come to visit, her brothers help themselves to a blue apron with Thomas Train® characters. We all LOVE Grandpa's famous chocolate chip pancakes. They especially like it when he makes a large "L" for Liberty and "E" initials for the boys. Planning and prep involves food items for chocolate chip cookies made from the recipe on the back of a Nestlé's Semi-Sweet Chocolate Morsels® package. Secret tip from my mom's recipe: stir in one (1) cup of oatmeal before dropping by well-rounded half teaspoons onto greased cookie sheets.

Maybe we'll make a Chocolate Miracle Whip cake for someone's birthday, or mix up salad greens and other ingredients for dinner, or scrambled eggs (see recipes in back of book) for breakfast. Whatever our hands find to do, we always enjoy just being and working together. Even setting the table for the next meal gives us together time and lightens the load. Focusing an eager and young spirit is so gratifying. Simple words such as, "What a big help you are to me! What will Nana do when you go home? I won't have my good helper then."

> "Tell me and I forget. Teach me and I remember. Involve me and I learn," Benjamin Franklin.

- On a scale of 1-10 (10 being the highest level), how content are you with your looks? List features that you like? And list the ones you would like to change?
- Whom (if anyone) do you wish to catch their eye or receive a favorable response/compliment from? Consider whether this expectation is proper or reasonable.
- What do the words fear the Lord mean to you? Write down a few ideas.

Day 77

I remember your genuine faith, for you share the faith that first filled your grandmother Lois and your mother, Eunice. And I know that same faith continues strong in you. This is why I remind you to fan into flames the spiritual gift God gave you when I laid my hands on you. For God has not given us a spirit of fear and timidity, but of power, love, and self-discipline— 2 Timothy 1:5–7/NLT.

What a precious heritage for those who have mothers and grandmothers, fathers and grandfathers of faith. I was privileged to have a mom who guided me in spiritual truths. My goal is to live a godly heritage and be that positive, spiritual mentor to my children and grandchildren. No dollar amount can be assessed to a spiritual legacy.

A pastor visiting one of his parishioners at the local hospital in Kentucky took an interest in my mom and dad when she gave birth to my younger brother, Lonnie. The pastor chatted with them and extended an invitation to visit his church. After a few frightening weeks of not knowing whether my brother would live or die, Pastor Maynard later visited my parents in our home after my brother was released from the hospital. During one of those home visits, mom and dad committed their hearts to Jesus. Over the years, my dad, siblings, and I witnessed a godly role model in my mom. Faith in action. Who could predict a simple act of kindness and an invitation to invite God into their lives could have such far reaching effects?

Paul, the missionary apostle, encourages us to keep the flames of faith alive. But we aren't left alone to our own devices. No, God provides the power, love, and self-discipline to accomplish those goals. The apostle Paul understood what was truly important in life. Encouraging others in the faith is not a one-time activity, but an ongoing process. Stand courageously for the truth even when exhausted. Prepare to see few rewards or differences and receive little or no praise for our efforts. Not a simple assignment, yet not impossible. In His strength. God's work continues behind the scenes. Here are a few relevant suggestions for keeping faith alive:[45]

- Memorize key passages in the Bible for immediate recall
- Listen to Scripture and how it might impact our lives
- Study Scripture intently for special counsel
- Read the Bible regularly to recognize God's viewpoint

"Visit many good books, but live in the Bible," Charles H. Spurgeon.

- Think back to a godly ancestor and record their significance to you.
- What is the definition of mentor? Name one or two individuals whom you could mentor spiritually. Who in your life could be (or already is) a spiritual mentor to you?
- What do you need to do in order to *fan into flames the spiritual gift God gave you*?

Day 78

People were bringing little children to Jesus for him to place his hands on them, but the disciples rebuked them. When Jesus saw this, he was indignant. He said to them, Let the little children come to me, and do not hinder them, for the kingdom of God belongs to such as these. Truly I tell you, anyone who will not receive the kingdom of God like a little child will never enter it. And he took the children in his arms, placed his hands on them and blessed them— Mark 10:13–16.

In the passage above, Jesus reminds us that in order for anyone to enter the kingdom of God, they must become like a child. He loves children and desires their protection from harm. When I think of the word child, these words come to mind: innocence, honesty, trust, humble, obedient, and teachable. This is how Jesus wants us to come to Him … in simple child-like trust. Knowing and believing that He is God and can save.

Words count. Actions count. Children are like sponges soaking up every word and action. I am fortunate to have young people in my life. Two children, four grandchildren to date, nieces and nephews all compose what I classify as young and impressionable. As a wife, mom, grandmother, sister, aunt, and great aunt, my standards should be high. Others watch and mimic my behavior. I do not want to be guilty of leading anyone astray. Anyone abusing these little ones will incur God's wrath. Whoever causes one of these little ones to stumble and sin, *it would be better for him to have a great millstone fastened around his neck and to be sunk in the depth of the sea* (Matthew 18:6/AMP).

Parenting is not for the faint of heart. Neither is being a proper role model. The job takes perseverance and courage. The task remains ongoing beyond the time they move out from under our roof. Needs and problems manifest themselves differently, but they still need to know we are available. Some responsibilities never change:

- Love them unconditionally (does not mean we approve of all their actions). Never give up loving them.
- Pray for them continually.
- Loveable hugs—reassuring touch conveys a feeling of belonging.

Ask and expectantly wait for God's wisdom. *And even when you ask, you don't get it because your motives are all wrong—you want only what will give you pleasure* (James 4:3/NLT). Even when asking, check that the motive is right and pure—not for selfish pleasure.

- What do the words *do not hinder the children* mean to you?
- Name the young people in your life whom you have influence over. Brainstorm and pray about how you can solidify godly commands to your children, grandchildren or any young people in your life.
- List ways you can be a positive role model for those young people? Now, plan to carry out a few of them.

Day 79

"I am here to live out loud!"—Emile Zola.

Anytime sickness or hospitalization enters the scene, there can be a nagging thought in the back of your mind. *Will I be restored to full health again? What if I'm not able to return home?* You might not voice your fears out loud. Maybe you speak those private thoughts to only one person.

My dear daughter planned a secret getaway refusing to tell me where we were headed. The only clue: don't wear white. We ended up sharing a fun-filled pottery adventure. She chose to paint a bright yellow happy sunflower with attached bumble bees. Then she presented her art creation back to me as a gift. I painted a frame for a picture of a bike trip Steve and I took. Overjoyed, I carefully brought my prize home. Afterwards, Amanda and I enjoyed a delectable dessert trio: fruit crème Brule, chocolate, and raspberry sorbet. Our wonderful evening completely took my mind off any medical issues.

Did I do everything right during those young, nurturing years? Of course not! But as my children grow older, I hope they realize I did my best in God's

Day 76-80   Little Eyes Watch

strength. I pray they will do the same when it comes time to have children of their own.

And you must commit yourselves wholeheartedly to these commands that I am giving you today. Repeat them again and again to your children. Talk about them when you are at home and when you are on the road, when you are going to bed and when you are getting up. Tie them to your hands and wear them on your forehead as reminders. Write them on the doorposts of your house and on your gates—Deuteronomy 6:6–9/NLT.

- What, if anything, do you wish you could change from your past? How can you make a positive difference in someone's life today? It's not too late to start now.
- Is your mind and heart at rest now? How do you know this is true?
- When and how did you last refill your own spiritual reservoir tank?

Day 80

"You must have been warned against letting the golden hours slip by. Yes, but some of them are golden only because we let them slip by,"
James M. Barrie.

Daydreaming. I am sometimes guilty of the opposite: not allowing myself time to daydream. Yet this quote from Barrie causes me to think differently about allowing my mind to wander. Barrie, the man who created Peter Pan and "granted him the pleasure of perpetual childhood surely knew the value of time.

I'm sure there were some who thought dreaming up fantasy adventures was a silly way for a grown man to spend his time—until he succeeded. Success has a way of validating silliness."

In those daydream moments, the unimaginable can happen. Pleasant images surface. Impractical hopes seem practical and attainable. Of course, daydreaming at inappropriate times when attention needs to be solely focused on something else is not recommended.

> *There is a time for everything, and a season for every activity under heaven:*
> *A time to be born and a time to die,*
> *a time to plant and a time to uproot,*
> *a time to kill and a time to heal,*
> *a time to tear down and a time to build,*
> *a time to weep and a time to laugh,*
> *a time to mourn and a time to dance,*
> *a time to scatter stones and a time to gather them,*
> *a time to embrace and a time to refrain from embracing,*
> *a time to search and a time to give up,*
> *a time to keep and a time to throw away,*
> *a time to tear and a time to mend,*
> *a time to be silent and a time to speak,*
> *a time to love and a time to hate,*
> *a time for war and a time for peace—Ecclesiastes 3:1-8.*

Children possess keen imaginations and think of unlimited ways to pass the time. They have a jolly good time playing with a simple cardboard box and playing games (while beating Nana). Even the youngest love to pretend by going grocery shopping or to the Farmer's Market to purchase ingredients for a meal. Who doesn't delight in fantasizing over make-believe tea parties? How refreshing to hear unrestricted, joyous laughter while swinging high, zipping down a slide, or building a legendary sandcastle. As we grow older, our minds think in more practical paths, a.k.a., boring circles.

> "Slow down parents! What's your rush anyway? Your children will be gone so quickly and you will have nothing but blurred memories of those years they needed you," Dr. James Dobson.

- When was the last time you climbed ladder rungs and sailed down a slide or clung tightly to the chains of a swing and pumped those legs for all you are worth? Put aside that pesky to-do list for a time. If it's been awhile, why not try something new and record your experience.
- Name a dream you have wanted to pursue, but never took the time to plan or ponder. Take time now to brainstorm.
- Talk to God about your dream and strategize together. Formulate a plan and record those thoughts.

Life is: Good Fragile Precious

Prayer of Encouragement:

Dear God, thank you for being with me. Especially the times when I'm uncertain about my next step. I come to You with open hands and an open heart. Ready for You to guide me through our next adventure. Even though it is scary, I know You are present. Help me filter through the many opportunities/distractions and be involved in only the best things You have in mind for me. Amen.

Read and meditate on the praiseworthy attributes of a virtuous woman found in Proverbs 31.

Day 76-80 Little Eyes Watch

Chapter 17

Dress-up Time

Put on therefore, as the elect of God, holy and beloved, bowels of mercies, kindness, humbleness of mind, meekness, longsuffering; forbearing one another, and forgiving one another, if any man have a quarrel against any: even as Christ forgave you, so also do ye. And above all these things put on charity, which is the bond of perfectness. And let the peace of God rule in your hearts ... and be ye thankful—
Colossians 3:12–15/KJV.

Chosen people. God's own hand-picked representatives. Wow! Those words imply volumes of thoughts. No randomness when God chose you and me. A deliberate choice made by the omnipotent and only wise God. That alone should dispel thoughts of inadequacy.

Earlier we talked about looking in the mirror to see what damage surgery had done. Even weeks later, I have no clue as to the extent of healing. I try not to ponder before the mirror. I did wake up in ICU and began breathing (with a bit of trauma). *Why am I here? Why did God choose me to live and others die?* The truth may never be known this side of heaven. This I cannot dwell upon. The focus needs to be on the here and now.

What should the well-dressed Christian wear or be concerned with? How fixated should we be on external appearances? Let's look at what to put on the inside before questioning how to adorn the outside. Paul, an apostle of Christ Jesus, gives us a few dress-up tips in Colossians 3:12–17.

- **Compassion, tenderhearted mercy.** Showing forth a heart of compassion or affection. This includes feeling sympathy or empathy for someone who is in need. Someone who could use a helping hand or a kind word. Having a strong desire to ease their suffering.
- **Kindness.** "Not merely goodness or kindness as a quality, rather it is goodness in action, goodness expressing itself in deeds."[46] Moral excellence (in character or demeanor). Showing love, doing a good deed. Making yourself friendly to someone without expecting any payback or retribution.

Put on your new nature, and be renewed as you learn to know your Creator and become like him (Colossians 3:10/NLT). Folks, we have our dress assignments. My conduct should match my faith. What I do and what I say should align with each other. "Because this process is lifelong, we must never stop learning and obeying ... there is an incentive to find the rich treasures of growing in him. It takes practice, ongoing review, patience, and concentration to keep in line with his will."[47]

"We draw people to Christ not by loudly discrediting what they believe, by telling them how wrong they are and how right we are, but by showing them a light that is so lovely that they want with all their hearts to know the source of it," Madeleine L'Engle.

- List a few habits from your old nature. Which of these are a struggle for you?
- What kindness have you received that evokes a strong memory? Write what happened.
- How do you rate on the moral excellence scale? Who has benefited from a compassion or kindness you showed them? List a few examples in your journal.

Prayer of Encouragement:

Dear God, help me not be so concerned with my outward appearance that I forget to take care of my inward character. May my appearance (inside and out) glorify You so that all will know I am a child of the King.

Day 81

Since God chose you to be the holy people he loves, you must clothe yourselves with tenderhearted mercy, kindness, humility, gentleness, and patience. Make allowance for each other's faults, and forgive anyone who offends you. Remember, the Lord forgave you, so you must forgive others. Above all, clothe yourselves with love, which binds us all together in perfect harmony. And let the peace that comes from Christ rule in your hearts. For as members of one body you are called to live in peace. And always be thankful—Colossians 3:12-15/NLT.

Day 81-85   Dress-up Time

Which of these character trait pieces of clothing do you struggle with most? Are there some in this grouping that come naturally to you and your personality? God's mercies are new every morning. He is pleased when we exhibit an attitude of gratitude. God desires me to present myself holy for all to see. Here are a few more ways to clothe this body while carrying out His mission:

- **Humility**. Humbleness of mind. Putting my neighbor before myself. *And all of you, dress yourselves in humility as you relate to one another, for God opposes the proud but gives grace to the humble. So humble yourselves under the mighty power of God, and at the right time he will lift you up in honor,* as described in 1 Peter 5:5–6/NLT. Having a modest, appropriate opinion of one's own importance or rank. We all know someone, who by obvious non-verbal body language, tells the world they are extremely proud. Maybe it is the way he sticks his chin out, rolls the eyeballs, or crosses his arms. Picture Christ dying on the cross as the ultimate example of true humility.

- **Meekness or gentle ways.** "Grace of the soul; and the exercises of it are first and chiefly towards God. It is that temper of spirit in which we accept His dealings with us as good, and therefore without disputing or resisting … it is equanimity of spirit that is neither elated nor cast down, simply because it is not occupied with self at all." (*Vine's Dictionary*) Meekness does not equal weakness, but is quiet strength under control. Humbly being patient even when treated unfairly. We want what is fair and what's coming to us. Stinking thinking believes this can only be accomplished through railroading our desires. Not according to these verses in Colossians.

We dare not lose heart. Our outward body appears to be wasting away, *yet inwardly we are being renewed day by day. For our light and momentary troubles are achieving for us an eternal glory that far outweighs them all. So we fix our eyes not on what is seen, but on what is unseen, since what is seen is temporary, but what is unseen is eternal* (2 Corinthians 4:16–18). Many questions surface, *will I always be dependent on someone else for food and simple mobility? Will I return to status quo?* I am leaning on the fact that God is too good to be unkind and too wise to make mistakes.

"Joyfulness is the foundation crème. A smile—the finishing touch," Unknown.

- How do you rate on the humility scale using 1-5 as your guideposts (1 being the least humble; 5 for a great amount of humbleness)? Are you satisfied with that number? Ideas on how to raise the score?
- What type of circumstances or people do you have trouble being gentle around?
- In what ways have you exhibited meekness or gentleness recently? List one or two examples.

Day 81-85   Dress-up Time

Day 82

"Faith is the bird that sings while it is yet dark," Max Lucado.

Waiting. Patiently. Patience does not come naturally to most people. I grow weary in praying for the same thing over and over. If I prayed for something over an extended period of time, shouldn't that request magically appear? Being committed to prayer involves time and work. Caring for others and our own body takes work. Hard work. I have a follow up appointment with my reconstructive eye surgeon, the one who worked alongside my neurosurgeon. The week before I needed extensive eye tests to evaluate my current status. My surgeon says my eyes look good. The results show I am seeing well too. Good news to hear. Why can't future testing be eliminated? Unfortunately, that's not the way the process works. Interesting that the next piece of clothing to investigate is:

- **Longsuffering (patience).** Fortitude. "Longsuffering is that quality of self-restraint in the face of provocation which does not hastily retaliate or promptly punish; it is the opposite of anger and is associated with mercy ..." (*Vine's Dictionary*). Bearing with one another in love. Waiting on something or someone with a calm, gracious spirit. Even when it takes longer than you originally intended. Without complaint or loss of temper, quiet steady perseverance. Patience with someone's immaturity or lack of knowledge involves tireless stamina with the power to endure. Whew! That sounds like a huge act to follow. Sometimes I want what I want, and I want it right now.

I have not been outside for two long days. The weather remains frigid; cold air blows without end. Today, I would love to walk outdoors and clear the cobwebs in my brain. Instead, I wrap my handmade shawl tightly around me. My shawl came with this message:

"This healing shawl is a gift to you created by a friend. Each time the needles and yarn were picked up to work on this shawl, she prayed: Creator God, may this shawl be a sign of Your healing presence; may it warm those who are weary, surround those who suffer and encircle those who are in pain. May Your gentle touch reach out to heal in the name of Christ.
We pray that the warmth of this prayer shawl will bring you a sense of God's peace, healing, and love each time you wrap it around your shoulders."

- In what circumstances and in what ways do you feel comforted? List them in your journal.
- How easy does being patient come for you? What are you waiting on? Or maybe you're waiting for someone to act in a certain way. If so, whom?
- Does your faith sing in the dark? If so, think of a circumstance when it did. Record that memory.

Day 83

"Holding onto anger is like drinking poison and expecting the other person to die," Felice Dunas

Along with this celebratory month of December can also come a season of downright depression. Past negative experiences often tarnish the otherwise festive event. Loss of my mom, Steve's dad, and grandparents remind us of the brevity of life. We mourn the empty spots around the table.

There is also the flip side; not all family members may be considered loved ones. I think of them as irregular people. I'm guessing we all have one or more irregular people in our immediate sphere of influence. This is the season of year when we are expected to gather with family. Presenting a happy face is not always realistic for whatever reason. Putting on a garment of forgiveness requires resilience in the face of great determination. I, too, am a work-in-progress. Key to survival: remember how the Lord forgives over and over again. He is our role model to follow.

- **Be gentle and forbearing with one another**. To hold up, to bear or suffer with. Coming alongside someone physically at a time not necessarily convenient for me. It may mean attaching oneself emotionally and spiritually by praying for someone's specific need.

- **Forgiving one another**. To bestow a favor unconditionally. Pardon, rescue or deliver. Freely giving, not expecting anything in return. You mean I need to forgive anything anyone has ever done? Even if that something is horrendous? Only through

God and His supernatural strength is this possible. Time and seeking God's wisdom go a long way in this huge task. This may mean forgiving someone who has not even asked us to forgive them. Lack of forgiveness is similar to anger, an acid "that can do more harm to the vessel in which it is stored than to anything on which it is poured."[48] In the book of Colossians, we read, *bearing graciously with one another, and willingly forgiving each other if one has a cause for complaint against another; just as the Lord has forgiven you, so should you forgive* (Colossians 3:13/AMP). In other words, keep short accounts.

"A personal insult becomes an opportunity for a saint to reveal the incredible sweetness of the Lord Jesus … never look for righteousness in the other person, but never cease to be righteous yourself," Lucius Annaeus Senecca.

"Life appears to me too short to be spent in nursing animosity or registering wrongs," Charlotte Bronte.

You may be thinking, but what if that other person deserves to be tongue lashed or worse? What if they respect nothing I say or do? What then? Don't they warrant being treated the same way they treated me? According to Scripture, the answer is no. We should not treat them the same way as they treat us. We should treat them better, go the extra mile and turn the other cheek (Matthew 5:38–40).

"To forgive is to set a prisoner free and discover that the prisoner was you," Lewis B. Smedes.

- Is there someone you cannot get out of your mind because they have wronged you so deeply? Name that person. Go to God pouring your heart out telling Him your grief. Ask what you should do. Then, go, say and do what He reveals to you. This is by no means an easy task.
- Think of someone with whom you have a challenging time being around (he/she may even be a family member). Consider why.
- Consider praying for this person. Ask for God's help to see this individual through His eyes; not through your own finite lens. "God gives us discernment in the lives of others to call us to intercession for them, never so that we may find fault with them ... Vicarious intercession means that we deliberately substitute God's interests in others for our natural sympathy with them."[49]

Day 84

For you are great and do marvelous deeds, you alone are God. Teach me your way, O Lord, and I will walk in your truth; give me an undivided heart, that I may fear your name. I will praise you, O Lord my God, with all my heart; I will glorify your name forever—Psalm 86:10–12.

Thank you, Lord, for decreased headaches yesterday and today. Weaning down the pain medications; this is good news. Wondering, *are we gaining ground, getting closer to no pain meds? This does not mean I don't want to depend on You, but I do grow weary of leaning on medications and other people.*

Learning to receive life differently these days. Part of this new mindset has been imposed on me and part of it, I am choosing.

- Slower pace. Less worry, less scurry, less flurry. Stop and smell the roses along the path.
- Simplify life. Less complicated. Enjoy what I have. Enjoy the basics.
- Savor life and every moment!
    - Forget and not dwell on yesterday.
    - Fret not about tomorrow.
    - Live in present mode. Today.

Last, but not least, charity or love. "Christian love, whether exercised toward the brethren, or toward men generally, is not an impulse from the feelings, it does not always run with the natural inclinations, nor does it spend itself only upon those for whom some affinity is discovered." (*Vine's Dictionary*) Love: Greek word is "agapē," which means a God-given love, benevolence, dear. Above all these things, put on or clothe self with the garment of love. Love binds everything completely together in ideal harmony or unity. If all else fails, love does not fail. *Beyond all these things put on and wrap yourselves in* [unselfish] love, *which is the perfect bond of unity* [for everything is bound together in agreement when each one seeks the best for others] (Colossians 3:14/AMP).

According to Paul, the writer of the book of Colossians, my thought patterns and sights should be on heavenly things; not entirely on the things of this earth. The things of this earth will grow strangely dim and I'll care less and less about them the older I become.

Day 81-85   Dress-up Time

- Are you able to show love freely? To whom is it easy to show love? Whom is it difficult to show love?
- Consider what an undivided or pure heart would look like.
- List some ways to put on or clothe yourself with love. Formulate a prayer back to God asking Him to clothe you in love or charity.

Day 85

Since you have been raised to new life with Christ, set your sights on the realities of heaven, where Christ sits in the place of honor at God's right hand. Think about the things of heaven, not the things of earth. For you died to this life, and your real life is hidden with Christ in God. And when Christ, who is your life, is revealed to the whole world, you will share in all his glory—Colossians 3:1–4/NLT.

Paul adds two more tidbits which packs a big punch when implemented properly:

- **Peace**. *And let the peace that comes from Christ rule in your hearts. For as members of one body you are called to live in peace* (Colossians 3:15/NLT). To rule means to govern, to arbitrate. Peace should have the upper hand in all dealings with people. As much as it depends on me, peace should be a common goal.

- **Thankful.** Greek word for "ĕucharistŏs,"—well favored, grateful. Gracious, agreeable. *Let the peace of Christ* [the inner calm of one who walks daily with Him] *be the controlling factor in your hearts* [deciding and settling questions that arise]. *To this peace indeed you were called as members in one body* [of believers]. *And be thankful* [to God always] (Colossians 3:15/AMP).

The idea being that we seek to always be thankful and give praise to God. I am a work in progress with God at the helm. As one season gives way, another marches forward:

> **Pressing On**
> Gentle dusting of light snowflakes
> Covers brownish-green earth's top layer
> Disappearing fall leaves
> Little remains green
> New season
> New chapter
> Off with the old
> On with the new
> New lease on life
> White veil signals brand-new days
> Forgetting what lies behind
> Straining toward what comes ahead
> Press on toward the goal
> To win the prize to which
> God has called me[50]

Day 81-85   Dress-up Time

- What does it mean to you to live the new life? Think about your life's progression. Go back one month, six months, a year, and beyond. How are you living your life differently? If you have not been living the life you had hoped and dreamed, what steps can you take to get closer to this goal?

- Name some people/things you are thankful for in your life. When life becomes stressful (and it will if it isn't already), go back to your journal and rehearse these lines.

- What changes should you make in order to be well-dressed and outfitted for active duty in this world? After contemplating this, fashion your answer back to God in the form of a prayer. Nothing fancy. Just you and God.

Prayer of Encouragement:

   Dear God, I try to comply with these wardrobe characteristics. I try; I fail. But when I rely on You, Your strength comes through every time. When I stumble and fall (and I will time and time again), You cover me with mercy, kindness, and forgiveness. The same qualities I need to show my neighbor. Thank You for hiding me safe within Your arms here on earth. I look forward to what You have in store for me in heaven as well. All in Your perfect timing.

Challenge: Meditatively read Colossians 3. Think through any new information you plan to incorporate in your life.

Grandson Elijah

Chapter 18

Choosing Joy

The cheerful heart has a continual feast—Proverbs 15:15b.

    Isn't it easier to exude gloom and doom and soak in misery? The cheerful heart is a continual choice. Sometimes it takes less effort to notice the negatives and ignore the positive blessings. *A miserable heart means a miserable life; a cheerful heart fills the day with song* (Proverbs 15:15/MSG). Most days, it's a matter of **choosing** to be joyful—a choice to fill the day with song and thanksgiving to the Almighty.

Someone's life is upside down no matter which way I turn. Unplanned teen pregnancy, addiction struggles, and death. Despair, low self-esteem, denial and lies touch many families. When someone's heart is broken, my heart breaks too. I long to fix problems, repair wounds, and put the happy picture back together again. Yet only God is able to fully restore. Paul gives us valuable insight/guidelines when dealing with others, *Rejoice with those who rejoice; mourn with those who mourn.* [51]

After experiencing an emotional week with an unemployed family member, a friend phoned and wanted to chat. My patience wore thin and my stinking attitude came through loud and clear. What was happening around me was not my friend's fault. Thankfully, she accepted my apology, but I knew it was time to take a walk and dust the cobwebs off my brain (again). Fresh air and exercise helped me regroup.

A continual feast takes energy. Uncertain financial times and health problems do not naturally equate a cheerful heart. Quite the opposite. Am I exempt from exhibiting a *cheerful heart* when the doctor discovers a brain tumor? What human being would jump for joy and shout, "Guess what? I may have cancer, or at the very least, may lose my eyesight!"

A *continual feast* takes faith in the God who created me. He knows my every weakness and still loves me. I must choose to trust in what cannot be seen, but still exists. Supernaturally, through the Holy Spirit, I can rejoice and look for glass half full implications. Those qualities will not necessarily change the circumstances, but having a good attitude and proper focus will help me handle life joyfully.

Life is: Good Fragile Precious

"What we see depends mainly on what we look for,"
British statesman John Lubbock.

- What blessing do you need to pause and record in your journal?
- Who can you share this blessing with and rejoice together?
- Is there someone who needs a few extra minutes of your time today? Who is that person and how can you infuse a little joy into their life?

Prayer of Encouragement:

Dear God, I realize there is no benefit in worrying myself into a deep ditch due to circumstances and other people's problems. Open my eyes to the good things in my everyday life. Fill this day with a song brought on by a cheerful heart as I rely on You as my source of strength and joy. Allow joy to radiate from me while encouraging others to look for the positives and trust in You.

Day 86

A happy heart makes the face cheerful, but heartache crushes the spirit—
Proverbs 15:13.

A cheerful heart brings a smile to your face; a sad heart makes it hard to get through the day—Proverbs 15:13/MSG.

Day 86-90   Choose Joy

What brings you joy? Take a few minutes to read responses to that question in the section marked What Gives You Joy? and then jot down your thoughts. I wanted them easy to find and refer to for instant inspiration. You and I represent uniquely, wonderfully made individuals. What causes joy for one person may not touch another the same way. I discover joy in the silliest and smallest of things. Steve claims, "It doesn't take much to amuse some people!" And I'm okay with that declaration. I envision where I would not mind being locked up overnight. Several locations surface immediately: a bookstore (with coffee, food, and a comfortable sofa), office supply store or a library. Time stands still when I visit those types of stores. Each aisle or section offers much to peruse, meditate and dream about.

When we smile and laugh, less wrinkles form than from scowling. Consider smile wrinkles badges of courage and a reward for living a good life. *She is clothed with strength and dignity; she can laugh at the days to come* (Proverbs 31:25/NIV). Are you prepared for the future? Can you say your family sees you laugh more than cry? Some days are harder than others. There are days I would rather stay in bed and never surface. Once I do rise and shine, the world seems a bit happier. And so am I. "Laughter lightens your load and lifts your heart into heavenly places."[52] Will you decide to go forth and find joy in each new day and setting?

Strength and dignity are her clothing and her position is strong and secure; and she smiles at the future [knowing that she and her family are prepared — Proverbs 31:25/AMP.

"Happiness comes when we stop complaining about the trouble we have, and say thanks to God for the troubles we don't have," Angela Rose.

- Do you find it tough to get through some days? You are not alone when you feel this way. What circumstance or events triggers sorrow?

- Name that sorrow while formulating a prayer to God telling Him your grief and asking that He bear the burden for you. He will do that, you know.

- What kinds of things/events/people cause you to smile giving you a joyful/cheerful heart? If you're happy, send your face that message so others will know too.

Day 87

The light of the eyes rejoices the hearts of others, and good news puts fat on the bones— Proverbs 15:30/AMP.

Sounds as though a person's attitude can be detected through their eyes—the window to the soul. I have a few people in my life who know when I am hurting and when I'm happy. Almost instantly. Some people can hide their emotions. I do not happen to be one of those people. I can fool some people, but usually not those closest to me.

Thankfully, my pain medications decrease as my body heals. I look forward to choosing my own destiny, or in this case, performing routine, normally mundane tasks on my own. In the past, I took for granted the items listed below and hurried to check the box.

- Writing at my home computer
- Organizing my home office space (STILL in progress project)
- Errand running
- Quality and quantity time with family and friends without tiring
- Being well

Good news grants health to your bones. *A twinkle in the eye means joy in the heart, and good news makes you feel fit as a fiddle* (Proverbs 15:30/MSG). Our bodies are complex and complicated. All the various parts connect and relate to each other. If our backs or feet ache, our face usually shows that pain. When we feel good and the people around us cause us joy, joy shows up on our face and on our lips too.

I'm happy from the inside out, and from the outside in. I'm firmly formed ... now you've got my feet on the life path, all radiant from the shining of your face. Ever since you took my hand, I'm on the right way—Psalm 16:9, 11/MSG.

- How vulnerable are you? Are you someone who hides their feelings? Which people in your life know you best?
- When someone looks into your eyes, what do they see? Do they see a twinkle in your eyes which means joy in the heart? *A cheerful look brings joy to the heart; good news makes for good health* (Proverbs 15:30/NLT).
- If you are not experiencing a twinkle in your eye or a spring in your step, what do you think is causing this? Stress, lack of sleep? Which people/circumstances makes it easier for you to be *happy from the inside out, and from the outside in?*

Day 88

Let us fix our eyes on Jesus, the author and perfector of our faith, who for the joy set before him endured the cross, scorning its shame, and sat down at the right hand of the throne of God. Consider him who endured such opposition from sinful men, so that you will not grow weary and lose heart—Hebrews 12:2–3.

Just as quickly, our face and heart can be crushed after receiving sad news. Feeling as if you cannot go on another day, possibly even another hour. I tried stepping aside and left my burdens alone for a short time. My headache and pain relax and subside. Slow down. Deep breaths. Close your eyes and bow your head. Inhale slowly for four counts, hold for four counts; exhale slowly. Silently count to four then repeat the inhale and exhale process. Recall thankful blessings and answered prayers.

Hallelujah, today's my last session with home physical therapists. Next, the discharge papers! Reading my devotional book and accompanying Bible verses, jotting down my thoughts, hopes, fears, and joys in my journal. Asking, *where am I now? Where do I need to be emotionally, physically, and spiritually?* Later in the day, I attend a church service where I meet many smiling faces. While expressing joy and praise to God, they remarked how good I looked. Venturing out proved the right action to take.

"Most folks are about as happy as they make up their minds to be,"
Abraham Lincoln.

- What/whom do you grow weary of in your life? Note how weariness affects other body parts. Take this burden to God in prayer.
- Go back to your journal of recorded verses. Find positive, uplifting ones telling of God's care and protection over you. Rehearse these promises often.
- Name a few things that are going well in your life. Find reason to praise and thank God for orchestrating those events/people into your life.

Day 89

You will show me the path of life; in Your presence is fullness of joy; at your right hand are pleasures forevermore— Psalm 16:11/NKJV.

I see my plastic and reconstructive surgeon today for another extensive eye exam. Even though people are praying for a good report, some apprehension still remains. The Apostle Paul's words come to mind, *God hath not given us the spirit of fear; but of power, and of love, and of a sound mind* (2 Timothy 1:7/KJV). I choose to repeat those comfort words over and over in my mind and speak them out loud. Hold fast to them and record them in my journal.

Good news: my reconstructive surgeon reports that I am healing as expected. This process still needs time, but he listed no limitations. My vision is excellent with some permanent swelling to be expected. He told me farewell and see you in a few months for additional, ongoing testing.

Christmas and the holidays approach. It takes extra discipline to not over-do. Feeling somewhat numb to this busy, rush season, I refuse to get caught up in the hustle-bustle. I must rest and ponder the real reason for the season: Jesus. Driving on my own, I checked out various stores for Christmas gifts. I felt free and independent once again. At one of my favorite consignment shops, I met the owner's mother and mentioned my brain surgery. She shared with me that years ago, her father had a similar craniotomy. He spent a month in the hospital and months in recovery afterward. Her father lived to be 90 years old.

"I never would have guessed you recently had brain tumor surgery. How well you've recovered from the surgery!" commented the store owner.

"God and my prayer warriors fought the battle. The whole situation is a God-thing and I'm here today because of the grace of God." I replied.

Happiness[53]

One of the big differences between sad people and happy people is that sad people become negative evidence collectors, dutifully looking for AWFUL things, people, and events to put into a mental folder labeled PROOF LIFE IS AWFUL.

Happy people are positive evidence collectors, constantly looking for positive things to put into a mental folder labeled, PROOF LIFE IS AWESOME. Because happy people collect AWESOME not AWFUL stuff, they notice and attract more AWESOME stuff, thereby filling up their mental folders with lots of happy evidence which further proves that yes indeed life is AWESOME.

- Which of these two people are you? Be honest. Do you look for awful things to collect and be filed in a Proof Life is Awful folder? On the flip side, what positive things have you accumulated for your positive evidence collector? How full is your Proof Life is Awesome folder? Which folder collects more evidence?
- Do you have a sense of where your life is headed? What do you feel is your purpose in life?
- Have you felt the presence and leading of God? If so, what did this feel like?

Day 90

Above all else, guard your heart, for it is the wellspring of life for everything you do flows from it—Proverbs 4:23.

My interpretation: just let it go! Many came alongside me during trying days sharing gifts of love, hugs, meals, and kind words. The looming question remains in my head: *will I always be dependent on others?* Probably not, but when you reside smack dab in the middle of a situation, it feels like an eternity. Maybe you have been there, or are currently in this state. Even when motivation is not present; praise God anyway.

Thank you, God, for not being too busy to pay attention to details, situations, and people. You have eyes to see and ears that listen to my heartache. You send people on Your behalf to comfort and encourage the weak. Sometimes we ask, and sometimes You just send them to us out of Your gracious, giving heart. All (my family and I, plus the person who shares) benefit when we allow others to help.

Today I see the main neurosurgeon who performed my surgery. My body is still moving slower than before surgery. Frequent rests are needed, but I am praising God for daily progress. We want change effective immediately. Change does not usually happen that way. I am thankful for progressive baby steps. My neurosurgeon tells me healing continues better than expected. This is great news! God answers prayers. Every day my strength increases as I rest, do a few tasks, and rest again.

"It is not happy people who are thankful; it is thankful people who are happy," Unknown.

- Look up the definition for the word guard. Think of several ways to guard or keep your heart safe from harm or danger. Journal your own personal protection plan. Note: Due to a recent unpleasant encounter, I was having a hard time functioning. Tears began to roll. I called my friend who kindly re-reminded me to guard my heart. *Above all else, guard your heart, for everything you do flows from it* (Proverbs 4:23). Protect and hold your heart close.

- Focus your attention on God and all the good He has bestowed on you, on your family. Mediate on those good things and formulate a prayer back to God.

- What ways have you learned to walk in God's truth through this study? Which method will you put into practice? Brainstorm ideas in your journal.

Life is: Good Fragile Precious

Prayer of Encouragement:

Dear God, this has been a miraculous journey! You and me and Your praying people. I am ready to move on in Your strength. Thank you for the many answers to prayer—too numerous to count. You are the giver of all good and perfect gifts. All the glory and honor belongs to You. Bless those in my life who sacrifice their time, energy, and prayers. They have blessed and touched our lives in ways I may never know. Help me remember to live in the present and not project myself too far in the future. You've got my life situation under control. I do not want to go back to who I was pre-surgery; I'm sticking with the new and improved Teresa. I will trust and obey You for as long as You choose me to be a light on this earth. Amen.

Challenge: Read through Proverbs 15 (in the translation of your choice) and begin your list of positive evidence collectors. Label your folder: Proof Life is Awesome. (See Day #89 for details)

Life is: Good Fragile Precious

NOTES

The Velveteen Rabbit[54]

"You become. It takes a long time. That's why it doesn't happen often to people who break easily, or have sharp edges, or who have to be carefully kept. Generally, by the time you are Real, most of your hair has been loved off, and your eyes drop out and you get loose in the joints and very shabby. But these things don't matter at all, because once you are Real you can't be ugly, except to people who don't understand."

Parting Words

Come to Me, all who are weary and heavily burdened [by religious rituals that provide no peace], and I will give you rest [refreshing your souls with salvation]. Take My yoke upon you and learn from Me [following Me as My disciple], for I am gentle and humble in heart, and you will find rest (renewal, blessed quiet) for your souls. For My yoke is easy [to bear] and My burden is light—Matthew 11:28–30/AMP.

Today, I'm not the same person who buried her head under the pillow upon hearing the voicemail about my MRI results. I walk this path for a reason and dare not waste valuable lessons lived and learned. Growth and maturity could not be achieved without having looked death straight in the eye.

Thankfulness and reliance on God brought me through suffering and recovery times, even when I did not feel like being thankful. Instead I chose thankfulness and witnessed miracles and answers to prayer. Now I can actually say that I am grateful for the learning experience. In every instance, doctors and medical staff showered me with care and patience. I sensed they felt a genuine vested interest in my well-being. I am most appreciative they chose to use their gifts and skills to serve and heal. Fortunately, the brain tumor proved to be a non-cancerous form called meningioma. Even though the doctors removed most of the tumor, there will be periodic MRIs and extensive eye tests to monitor potential further growth.

Last month I celebrated the big 60th birthday. The idea of a huge celebration came to me in the night. A few days later a level of embarrassment crept over me. I would need to announce that I am way past the number 50. Yikes! Then the other side of my brain chimed in with, *Isn't this silly to have a big to-do just for you. Think of the cost involved; is this really worth it?* Ever wrestle with both sides of an issue? I kicked those negative thoughts right out and went forth with the plans. Thoughts of celebration soon superseded monetary issues and the pride of admitting my age. Why not celebrate 7 years post brain surgery AND 60 years of living and life?

Over 50 family members and friends came from near and far for my birthday bash; just for me and my party, imagine that! My son and family drove almost 700 miles just to be with me for the weekend. For those who could not attend the party, we celebrated individually later. This fantastic, fun occasion produced blessings beyond measure. And to think, I nearly cancelled the idea! A beachy theme included delicacies such as Boiled Octopus (pulled pork), Coral Reef Salad (Italian pasta), Beach Glass (fresh fruit salad), and Fish Eyeballs (large green olives). Following the pomp and circumstance, decorations came down and people went home, I sat to muse on the festivities. These words bubbled forth from my heart:

Birthday Celebration and Beyond

Family and friends gather

Form a beautiful tapestry

of God's love and mercy

Together we walk, talk, eat, drink, and pray

Intertwined in one another's lives

Common threads link us

Thanking Him for another 7 years on earth

After frightful brain surgery

Much to be thankful for & celebrate

I love all of you and

am so proud of you

Each a unique gift from God

> You've touched my life
> In a special, individual way
> A gift which cannot be bought, boxed
> Or tied with ribbon or bow
> Thank you for giving the gift of yourself
> Being present

I still struggle to do what is right in this on-going process toward wellness and restoration. We all wear the title: Works-in-Progress. Think of life as a marathon (long-distance prolonged effort deserving attention and endurance) vs. a sprint (short-term race at your highest running speed). Pace yourself for roadblocks and detours. Along your travel route, you will encounter speed bumps which may or may not look like mine.

My favorite quote bears repeating: Let go and let God. Deep breaths, my friend. Watch and wait for God to show up; it's always worth the wait! Zero in on a few lessons or ideas encountered within these pages. Set realistic goals for yourself. Remember, baby steps—one step at a time achieves more than you think. "The secret to success is making very small, yet, very consistent, changes. Or, to make it short, baby steps, baby steps in the right direction. Never underestimate the inevitability of gradualness."[55] Albert Einstein reminds us that, "Life is like a bicycle—in order to keep your balance, you must keep moving."

Life is Good

Life is Fragile

Life is Precious

Live life exuberantly in the present

Blessings from a fellow-pilgrim/traveler,

Teresa K. Lasher
Jeremiah 29:11–13

P.S. I'd love to hear your story about struggles with proper self-care, learning to live in the present, or whatever you would like to discuss. Feel free to share your story. Contact me through our website at www.LasherArts.com where Steve and I blog about our travels and photography adventures.

What gives you joy?

"Seeing my Nana/Grandmas, Grandpas and family." (my dear granddaughter Liberty).

"Spending time with my husband, kids, grandkids and friends. Also, answered prayer …. we have had a lot of those this last month. Feeling the peace that passes all understanding." (Bonnie)

"Fishing, being outside in God's creation." (my son Andrew)

"Something very simple …. I love spending time with my nephews. I love hearing them ask questions, laugh those big hearty belly laughs. I love getting their hugs when they run up to see me or hear them finish the sentence, 'I love you … to the moon and back Auntie Kim.' Knowing I can make a small difference in their lives is a good thing." (Kim)

Some find great joy in cooking or baking. Others enjoy their animals or "sweet kitties" (Katelyn) and walks in the great outdoors.

"Family, kids, grandkids, smell of lilacs, the smell of the ocean, sound of the waves, hearing a favorite song, camping, playing games together, hot summer days, cooking, baking, a roaring fire." (my sister Karen)

Sharry writes, "A dear sister-friend who loves me unconditionally and someone I can always count on. Grandkids who all want to sit next to me, but I have only two sides. Mostly what gives me joy is my salvation. Love and affection of those who love and appreciate me (and tell me so). I truly felt the Lord's hug while in the pre-op room alone and scared about my surgery. I'll never forget it because it was real and true."

From Brian, "I feel joy when I feel God's presence. I often feel God's presence in my wife, children, friends, co-workers and through my writing. The writing connects me with God and my Soul and helps me see myself and the world through God's perspective. Yeah God!!"

My daughter Amanda, "It gives me joy to be able to brighten someone's day or help them when they least expect it. Joy is that unforgettable "aha" moment when you're spending time with loved ones and you realize these moments are what life is all about. Joy is the sparkle in my mom's eyes when she sees me walk through the doorway or when she squeals with excitement when she opens the present I thoughtfully picked out for her."

"Joy to me is: Jesus loves me this I know for the Bible tells me so." (Jan)

"There are so many things to enjoy if you look for them. I really enjoy watching students at the moment they 'get it,' that moment you see in their eyes that it just clicked and now makes sense. The pride that follows is almost as awesome." (Cinnamon)

My writer-friend Noreen writes, "Joy comes in small things. Pink and white tulips, I drove by a stranger's yard and spotted blossoming apple trees ... Lilac bushes budded. New hosta in our yard transplanted from my sister's yard, originally from our Mom's yard."

"My garden. It's like a marriage of God and me. He allows me to tend His creation and then blesses it with Spiritual application with His Word. Planting. Waiting. Bearing fruit. Faithfulness. Beauty ... I found joy in loss, which I suppose means loss of control, and that God is in control." (Joy)

"Being with my family gives me joy. Thinking of all my blessings and how God helped me get through losing my mom. I don't know how I would have made it through that time without God." (Dory)

"I feel much joy when God answers my prayer in a way that I never would have thought of. He is all knowing and wise, His thoughts are not my thoughts; they are above and beyond anything I could ever imagine. It makes me want to leap with joy and shout for all to hear. He is real, He is real, and God is real!!!" (Jody)

My nephew Jeremy, "Making people smile and be happy because of what I do/say. Simple notes and surprises in school locker or texts ... letting other people know you care."

"Ballet... To me it's not just dancing, it's an extension of worship. It's a way I can express my innermost feelings that can't be expressed with words. (daughter-in-law Bethany)

"My almost-three-year-old granddaughter telling me how much she loves Jesus." (Sherry)

"As I child, I remember learning in junior church to put **J**esus first, **O**thers second, **Y**ourself last—to have **J. O. Y.** It works!" (Janet)

"Squishy hugs from Maddie and listening to Kayleigh quote Bible verses in Mandarin." (Deb)

Former college classmate, Marissa, responds with, "I love family time, as a group, and time spent individually with my husband & kids. I love time spent in nature: tent camping, bonfires under a starry sky, walking through the woods, walks on the beach, or swimming in the river. I also love my 'art therapy,'—sewing, making jewelry, cards, scrapbooking, and painting. These things rejuvenate and heal me."

"Toe touching with hubby." (Cynthia)

"I experience joy from friendly people who are walking in the park and smile directly at me and say either hi or something kind about my dog as we cross paths." (Mia)

"Riding my scooter always brings me joy. The best rides are the unplanned ones where I just pick a road and take off. Sometimes I get lost, but that's part of the fun." (Rachael)

"Sharing knowledge. Playing music well for someone who appreciates it. Helping someone through a difficult time." (David)

"I bet one moment of joy will be next week when I blow out the candles for my 90th birthday. I will be grateful for family, friends (many of whom are gone), and all of God's blessings." (Aunt Jackie)

"The time with my grandkids and my new great grandson!" (Simon)

"Hearing my granddaughter sing praises to our Lord!" (Shirley)

"Hearing my grandkids praying. So sweet and simple. Even James who is almost two, wants to pray before we eat. When asked who wants to pray and hearing all three grandkids say me, me, me. Love it. We have three grandkids living with us now." (Sharon)

"Hearing laughter!! Even when I see people laugh, it causes me to smile! It just warms my heart." (Rhonda)

"Hearing my 3-year old grandson say, 'I love you grandma.' Also, when my 6-month old grandson has an all-out belly laugh." (Margie)

"Spending time outdoors in nature, gardening, birdsong, every beloved companion animal that found its way to me, and laughing until I cry with my soulmate/husband and friends." (Cheryl)

"My family brings me joy and so does being outdoors!" (Cindy)

"My grandchildren, music, and my children." (Nancy)

"Seeing family happy and healthy. Sunny days. Ability to provide for my family." (Mike)

"Gaining someone's confidence and making them smile, trusting me, and see loss of fear leave their faces." (Paulette)

"Music. Hearing music gives me joy and can change my attitude immediately. The love of music is the greatest." (Jim)

Special Song

How Great Thou Art[56]

O Lord my God, when I in awesome wonder,
Consider all the worlds Thy Hands have made;
I see the stars, I hear the rolling thunder,
Thy power throughout the universe displayed!

Refrain:
Then sings my soul, my Savior God, to Thee:
How great Thou art, how great Thou art!
Then sings my soul, my Savior God, to Thee:
How great Thou art, How great Thou art!

And when I think, that God, His Son not sparing;
Sent Him to die, I scarce can take it in;
That on the Cross, my burden gladly bearing,
He bled and died to take away my sin!

When Christ shall come with shout of acclamation,
And take me home, what joy shall fill my heart!
Then I shall bow in humble adoration,
And there proclaim, my God, how great Thou art!

This song was the theme song for a week-long Vacation Bible School (VBS) at our Illinois church. During VBS, my sister and I asked Jesus to come into our hearts and life. I was 13; my sister, Karen, 11 years old. After singing that song and completing the daily activities, we both went home excited to tell the good news.

"We had one thing in mind: to share the most important decision in our life with the most important person in our life, our mom!" declares my sister.

We both chose to accept Jesus Christ as Savior the same day even though we were in different classes. At the time, we did not know the decision the other had made. Another God-thing. Later, we joyously entered the waters of baptism[57] together. Even today, many, many years later, this song still touches my heart and brings happy tears. *What if I hadn't said yes to God? Where would I be today?*

"What's becoming clearer and clearer to me is that the most sacred moments, the ones in which I feel God's presence most profoundly, when I feel the goodness of the world most arrestingly, take place at the table. The particular alchemy of celebration and food, of connecting people and serving what I've made with my own hands, comes together as more than the sum of their parts," Shauna Niequist, *Bread & Wine*

Recipes

Chocolate Miracle Whip Cake (from my mom, Jimmie Powders) [58]

Cream together:

1 cup Miracle Whip dressing

1 cup sugar

2 eggs (mom added eggs to the original recipe)

Stir together:

2 cups flour

2 teaspoons soda

4 tablespoons cocoa

1 dash salt

Beat dry mixture into the first ingredients alternately with:

1 cup cold water

2 teaspoons vanilla

Beat until smooth. Bake in 13" x 9" pan or two (2) cake pans at 350–degree about 30 minutes. Sometimes I sprinkle chocolate chips over the top about five minutes before cake is done; return to oven; swirl melted chocolate on top to form frosting. The melted chocolate gives a pleasant, interesting topping. Another method, after cooling, sprinkle with powdered sugar and serve. If you desire a traditional chocolate frosting, see below.

Frosting:

Melt together:

3 tablespoons cocoa

2 tablespoons margarine or butter

Beat in:

1 teaspoon vanilla

4 tablespoons milk

2 and ½ cups powdered sugar

Fresh, Basic, and Delicious Salad (shared by Nelli K.)

Lightly mix all together:

Boston lettuce/leafy green or red lettuce/spinach

Fruits of your choice (mango, strawberries, blueberries; whatever's fresh at the time, what you like/have on hand)

Cherry tomatoes

Basil or cilantro, if desired

Chopped, fresh avocado (top)

Mix of vinegar, oil* for the dressing (Fustini's oil recommended)

May add a touch of sugar (if desired, but not necessary)

Salt & pepper to taste

Lemon Bars (my favorite: Mom's recipe)[59]

1 cup butter or margarine

Pinch of salt

1/2 cup powdered sugar

2 cups flour

Blend all these and pat into a 9" x 13" pan. Bake in 350-degree oven for 20 minutes.

While this is baking, using fork, slightly beat together:

4 eggs

1 and 1/2 cup sugar

Juice and grated rind of two (2) lemons

Pour this on crust and bake additional 25–30 minutes. Cool, cut into squares. Dust with powdered sugar.

Scrambled Eggs [60]

Mix in a bowl:

4 eggs

¼ cup milk

½ teaspoon salt, scant

1/8 teaspoon pepper, scant

Heat in skillet:

1 tablespoon butter or margarine

Pour egg mixture in skillet until sides and bottom just begin to set. Gently lift cooked portions of egg with a spatula so the thin, uncooked part can go to the bottom of the skillet. Continue to lift and fold eggs gently until they are evenly cooked. DO NOT STIR. Cook until moist and glossy, about three (3) minutes. Top with shredded cheddar or your favorite cheese.

Pumpkin Muffins (shared by Gwen Lasher, mother-in-law)

4 eggs	2 cups sugar
1 and 1/2 cups oil	1 and 3/4 cup pumpkin (small can)
3 cups flour	1 tablespoon cinnamon
2 teaspoons baking powder	2 teaspoons baking soda
1 teaspoon salt	2 cups raisins

One-half recipe:

2 eggs	1 cup sugar
Scant cup pumpkin	1 and 1/2 cups flour
1 and 1/2 teaspoon cinnamon	3/4 cup oil
1/2 teaspoon salt	1 cup raisins (if desired)
1 teaspoon baking powder	1 teaspoon baking soda

Beat eggs slightly. Add sugar, oil, pumpkin and beat thoroughly. Add flour, cinnamon, baking powder, soda, and salt; mix until smooth. Stir in raisins. Fill greased muffins cups 3/4 full and sprinkle top with brown sugar. Bake at 375 degree 15-20 minutes. [Bake miniature about 14 minutes. This recipe makes 60 miniature muffins.]

I use the one-half recipe unless baking for a big crowd. Omit the sugar on top and raisins, if you prefer.

Tortellini Salad (shared by Lora C.)
3 cups uncooked cheese filled tortellini
2 cups fresh diced tomatoes
6 tablespoons extra virgin olive oil
6 fresh diced basil leaves (or 1/2 teaspoon dried)
1 cup cubed fresh mozzarella cheese
Salt and pepper to taste

Freshly grated Parmesan cheese
Spinach (added last minute)

In a large bowl, mix together: tomatoes, olive oil, basil leaves, cubed mozzarella cheese, salt and pepper. Cook tortellini according to package directions. Drain and add cooked tortellini to the mixture; cover and let set for a few minutes to melt cheese. Garnish with fresh parmesan cheese and serve either warm or cold.

Good Reads

Jesus Calling, Sarah Young. Modern day language helps focus on what really matters in this 365-day devotional.

My Utmost for His Highest, Oswald Chambers. Great daily devotional for moving nearer to God.

The Blue Zone, 9 lessons for living longer from the people who've lived the longest, Dan Buettner, National Geographic 11/2012. National Geographic author and his photographer traveled the globe to "uncover the best strategies for longevity found in the Blue Zone: places in the world where higher percentage of people enjoy remarkably long, full lives … unique lifestyle formula with latest scientific findings to inspire easy, lasting change that may add years to your life." In short, eat well, stress less, move more and love more.

Connect with the Author

The discovery of a brain tumor changed Teresa Lasher's life. These devotions/meditations reveal her walk with God as He healed her. In her new lease on life, she enjoys His creation while afloat with her husband aboard their boat, Sanctuary.

Besides speaking to various groups, she and Steve blog about their travels and share photographs of their adventures at: www.LasherArts.com. Teresa has written articles for magazines such as *Sailing*, *The War Cry*, *Rider*, *Women's Lifestyle*, and co-authored two pictorial travel books.

Life is: Good Fragile Precious

Endnotes

[1] Winnie-the-Pooh, also called Pooh Bear, created by English author, A.A. Milne

[2] "A Weekend to Change Your life—Find Your Authentic Self After a Lifetime of Being All Things to All People," by Joan Anderson, New York Times Bestseller author, Broadway Books, 2006

[3] Findings in *The State of Health in the American Workforce*, a report released by the Families and Work Institute (FWI)

Chapter 1

[4] Magnetic resonance imaging (MRI) is a test that uses a magnetic field and pulses of radio wave energy to make pictures of organs and structures inside the body. In many cases MRI gives different information about structures in the body than can be seen with an X-ray, ultrasound, or computed tomography (CT) scan. MRI also may show problems that cannot be seen with other imaging methods.

[5] A meningioma is a tumor that forms on membranes that cover the brain and spinal cord just inside the skull. Specifically, the tumor forms on the three layers of membranes that are called meninges. These tumors are often slow-growing. As many as 90% are benign (not cancerous). Most occur in the brain. But they can also grow on parts of the spinal cord. Often causing no symptoms and require no immediate treatment. But the growth of benign meningioma can cause serious problems. In some cases, such growth can be fatal.

[6] Elisha A. Hoffman, 1887

[7] Dobson, Ed, *Prayers & Promises when facing a life-threatening illness*, Zondervan, 2007

[8] ALS (Amyotrophic lateral sclerosis) often referred to as Lou Gehrig's disease. ALS is a progressive neurodegenerative disease that affects nerve cells in the brain and spinal cord.

Chapter 3

[9] Shared by Pastor Craig Cramblet, Olivet Evangelical Free Church

[10] small triangular sail in front of the mast on a sailboat

Chapter 4

[11] Point Betsie Lighthouse located on Lake Michigan shore

[12] Message on back of note cards from Papyrus paper company

[13] James Watkins, Hope & Humor, Writer, Speaker, Threat to Society, Indianapolis, Indiana, jameswatkins.com

[14] Craig McConnell

Chapter 5

[15] Brian Jacques (born June 15, 1939) made his style of writing as vividly descriptive as possible in his Redwall series. His first readers were the children of the Royal Wavertree School for the Blind.

Chapter 6

[16] 2 Chronicles 7:14/NLT

[17] Melchor Lim

[18] NIV Life Application notes

Chapter 7

[19] Sleeping Bear Dunes, 35-mile stretch of beautiful Lake Michigan's eastern coastline featuring immense sand dunes sculpted by winds and waters. Attractions: national park, forests, beaches, dune formations and glacial phenomena. http://www.michigan.org/property/sleeping-bear-dunes-lakeshore/

[20] *The Prayer of Jabez—Breaking Through to the Blessed Life,* by Bruce Wilkinson. Your prayer might go something like this: *O God and King, please expand my opportunities and my impact in such a way that I touch more lives for Your glory. Let me do more for You!*

Chapter 8
[21] Sarah Young, *Jesus Calling*, Thomas Nelson, 2004

Chapter 9
[22] Sarah Young, "Jesus Calling," March 15

[23] Poem by Robert Louis Stevenson, 1850-1894, Edinburg, Scotland. Source: Stevenson, R.L. (1913). *A Child's Garden of Verses,* Simon & Schuster

[24] Douglas MacArthur

[25] "Why Silence is So Good For Your Brain," Carolyn Gregoire, syndicated from *Huffingtonpost.com,* http://www.dailygood.org/story/1237/why-silence-is-so-good-for-your-brain-carolyn-gregoire/

Chapter 11
[26] Six Major Health Problems caused by Lack of Sleep - http://www.prevention.com/health/health-concerns/what-lack-sleep-does-your-body

[27] Quote from Matthew Walker, Berkeley professor of psychology and lead investigator of a study presented at the American Association of the Advancement of Science (AAAS) conference

[28] "The Hidden Danger of Nighttime Smartphone Use," by Sara Wylie

Chapter 12

[29] by Dan Buettner

[30] words from a Girl Scout campfire song

[31] To transgress/sin means "to step across" or "to go beyond a set boundary or limit." To "miss the mark" at which he was aiming. Encompasses going in one direction, but straying off course to the side and not continuing in the direction we intended to go, with the result that we don't reach the goal we intended. We miss; failing to measure up to a standard.

Chapter 13

[32] "My Utmost for His Highest," by Oswald Chambers, January 13

[33] For more insight into the tallit gadol, see: http://www.hebrew4christians.com/Blessings/Synagogue_Blessings/Donning_Tallit/donning_tallit.html

[34] O. Hallesby

[35] Joan Webb

36 Rick Warren, author of "Purpose Driven Life," shares choice words in an interview by Paul Bradshaw

Chapter 14

[37] Poet W. H. Auden, born February 21, 1907

[38] Cited in book entitled, "Just Enough Light for the Step I'm on—Trusting God in the Tough Times," by Stormie Omartian

[39] "Only Trust Him," text & music by John S. Stockton, The United Methodist Hymnal #337

Chapter 15

[40] Ottumwa, Iowa: Located in southeastern Iowa, the city is split into northern and southern halves by the Des Moines River. Also, home of Cpl. Walter Eugene "Radar" O'Reilly—fictional corporal and company clerk from the book, movie, and popular television series M*A*S*H. The town of Ottumwa is mentioned as Radar's hometown in the novel and regularly on the show.

[41] Lyrics from "How He Loves," by David Crowder Band

[42] Life Application Bible notes/NIV, Zondervan, referring to the book of Job

[43] *The Complete Works of E.M. Bounds on Prayer*, by E.M. Bounds

[44] Renceray Brown quote seen on church billboard by Mary M.

Chapter 16

[45] Quote taken from Jerry Bridge's book, "The Pursuit of Holiness."

Chapter 17

[46] From notes on Galatians, by Hogg and Vine, p. 292

[47] NIV Life Application Bible study notes

[48] Lucius Annaeus Senecca

[49] *Vicarious Intercession*/May 3 and 4 devotionals, Oswald Chambers, *My Utmost for His Highest*

[50] Thoughts and words from Philippians 3:12–14

Chapter 18

[51] Romans 12:15/NIV

[52] *Jesus Calling,* by Sarah Young, June 17

[53] Karen Salmansohn

[54] 1922 classic publication by Margery Williams

[55] Messies Anonymous Slogan, Sandra Felton

[56] "How Great Thou Art!" song written by Stuart K. Hine, born in 1899 in England. His parents were at that time worshipping with the Salvation Army, and dedicated him to God during a time when opposition was strong against those who proclaimed Christ. After serving in the Armed Forces, Mr. Hine was called to the mission field. For many years he served in Poland and Czechoslovakia. It was during missionary work in these countries that Mr. Hine composed many of the songs for which he's well-known today.

[57] Baptism: an outward expression or symbol of an inward decision/profession of faith in the Lord Jesus Christ. Just as water cleanses our physical bodies, baptism is a symbol of cleansing of the soul and heart by the Holy Spirit after becoming a Christian.

[58] Created lovingly by my mom, Jimmie Powders. I am uncertain as to the original source of the Chocolate Miracle Whip Cake recipe. Making and baking of this cake brings back many fond memories for us kids. Once a year for our birthday celebration, each of mom's children had the privilege of choosing a special cake she would create just for them. Whatever cake/dessert/main meal we chose, mom would diligently and lovingly prepare for us. We'd spend hours looking through her reliable red and white Betty Crocker® cookbook. In the end, we'd choose Chocolate Miracle Whip cake with chocolate frosting. No other cake compared. How can you improve upon chocolate on top of chocolate?

[59] Created lovingly by my mom, Jimmie Powders. Her famous, yummy, unbeatable Lemon Bars.

[60] Scrambled Eggs: one of the first recipes required to cook in my Home Economics class, junior high school, Sycamore, Illinois. My, that seems so long ago!

Made in the USA
San Bernardino, CA
27 June 2017